CHEAP WAYS TO...

By Jason Boyett, Margaret Feinberg
Josh Hatcher, and Katie Meier

Published by Relevant Books,
A division of Relevant Media Group, Inc.

www.relevantbooks.com
www.relevantmediagroup.com

© 2003 by Relevant Media Group, Inc.

For information:
RELEVANT MEDIA GROUP, INC.
POST OFFICE BOX 951127
LAKE MARY, FL 32795
407-333-7152

Library of Congress Control Number: 2002094145
International Standard Book Number: 0-9714576-4-6

03 04 05 06 9 8 7 6 5 4 3 2 1

Printed in the United States of America

CHEAP
WAYS
TO

TRAVEL. BUY A COMPUTER. ENTERTAIN. BUY A CAR. DECORATE. PLAN A WEI
HAVE A BABY. FIND A PET. GET A MASTER'S DEGREE. BUY CLOTHES. HELP THI

9 780884 197935

ENTER AINME T

CHEAP WAYS TO ENTERTAIN A TODDLER

By Jason Boyett

When couples find out they are pregnant for the first time, they do what all other parents do in the same situation: they start buying toys. Between lusting after Tickle-Me-Elmo to obsessions with the garage sale circuit, they figure they'll have baby's toy needs covered by the time he or she arrives. They soon learn what every parent learns in the first year, a lesson so prevalent it's become a cliché—kids aren't interested in the toy itself. What they're after is the box it came in. Babies aren't interested in colorful, mass-manufactured, tediously researched and developed toys for children. Nope. They want to play with rocks. Here are some cheap ways to entertain a toddler based on the preferences of my daughter, Ellie. Keep in mind that kids are unpredictable, to say the least. No guarantees that any of these will work, but don't let that stop you.

BOXES

What—you thought this first one would be something profound? No way. After Ellie's first birthday, we bought her one of those wiggly water sprayers for our yard. She played with the toy once, and lost interest after about five minutes. But the box? She played with the box every day until September, at which point it had become so trashed we had to throw it away secretly while she was napping. She stood in it. She hid crackers in it. She let her stuffed animals "sleep" in it. She kept it in her room, by her bed. It said it right there on the side of the box: "Hours of summer fun!" Who knew? It became her second favorite toy of the summer, next to …

Another box. This one was a big brown shipping box we lifted from my in-laws. My wife had the idea of turning it on its side, cutting windows in it, and decorating it like a house. With crayons, she drew curtains on the inside and flowers on the outside, and wrote Ellie's name prominently on the roof. Around the same time, Ellie discovered crayons herself, and she would spend large parts of each day climbing in and out of the box, coloring the cardboard walls and floor of her very own house. Her real toys gathered dust in a corner, forgotten. (There's a Pixar film somewhere in this.)

It doesn't have to be big boxes, either. For some reason—I'm assuming the one that compels children to pick up small objects—Ellie became infatuated with rocks that same summer. Gravel, landscaping stones, river rocks, anything she could get her hands on. She didn't throw them or eat them, as we expected. She just wanted to hold them. So we gave her an empty mints tin and taught her to open and close it herself. It became her rock box. She'd walk along our sidewalk, picking up loose pebbles and placing them in her tin. Then at night she'd open the lid, arrange the rocks inside, and close it up again. Cost: eighty-nine cents worth of mints.

COLORING

For most kids, there's really nothing better to occupy their time than a good art project. It's like discovering a new world once your toddler learns to hold a crayon and scrape it over a page. But don't go to the expense of buying fancy bound and printed coloring books for a two year old. A book will just get crumpled, spilled upon and generally destroyed. Instead, spend a couple of bucks on some nice, fat crayons—because the pictures don't matter much. What matters is a receptive surface.

To provide that, we've taken to recycling coloring surfaces (see the cardboard box example above). Ellie knows not to color on the walls, furniture, or herself, but anything else is fair game if she asks first. Once the newspaper's been read, it's ready to be scribbled on. Same for old magazines, paper grocery bags, junk mail, packing paper. If your toddler insists on structure to his coloring—i.e. an actual stay-inside-the-lines illustration—then turn on your computer. There are many, many websites for kids that feature printable coloring pages. If your kid likes Sesame Street, check out the coloring pages at *www.pbskids.org*, where you can choose a character, bring up a full-page illustration, and print it out. Disney characters can be found at *www.playhousedisney.com*. Go to Google.com and type in "coloring pages." You'll be surprised.

But crayons aren't the only cheap way to occupy a toddler's time. In the summertime, sidewalk chalk is a good way to do a little outdoor coloring. Because it washes away with water, any smooth surface is ideal. If you don't have your own sidewalk, head to a park. Keep some moist baby wipes on hand to clean off the dusty fingers afterward.

WATER

Here's another outdoor art alternative you may not have considered: water. We introduced Ellie to painting with water the summer after she turned two. It's easy. Buy a handful of cheap plastic paintbrushes (you can get several for less

1: TAN
2: LIGHT GREEN
3: MEDIUM GREEN
4: YELLOW
5: BROWN
6: BLUE

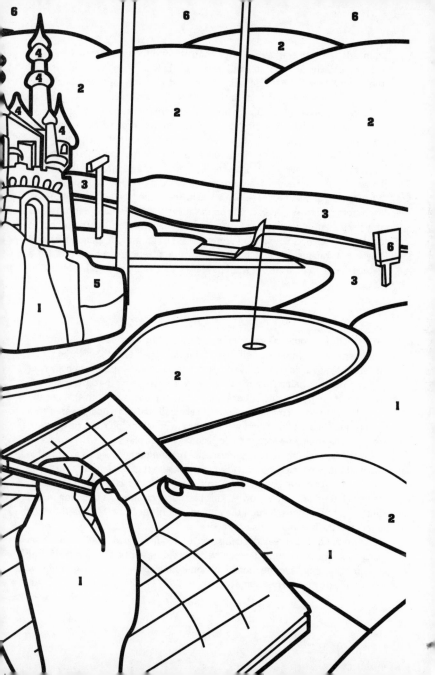

than a dollar from craft stores, supermarkets, or discount centers). Give your child a small cup of cold water and show them how to dip the brush in the cup, then "paint" it on the hot sidewalk. The water darkens the light concrete. On a hot day, you can usually get one or two minutes of good brushwork done before evaporation sets in. When that happens, find a dry spot and start over.

On a related note, something else we discovered early on with Ellie was that she liked pretend tea parties. Once her grandmother Jo-Jo showed her how to pretend sip and pretend pour, it was only a matter of time until Ellie began asking for a real beverage with her tea set. We were first-time parents; what did we know? We filled up her little tea pot with water, put her on a tile floor, grabbed a few towels, and let her loose. She loved it. She poured water from pot to cup, then from cup to cup, then from cup to saucer, then eventually back into the tiny tea pot. An endless cycle of water transfer, just like we all learned about in sixth grade science. The spilling decreased as she grew more coordinated, and anyway, it was just water. Ellie used an actual plastic tea set we found at a garage sale for a quarter, but she'd have been just as happy with a selection of Dixie cups.

TENTS

And finally, we come to every parent's old stand-by—the bed sheet tent. You could spend one hundred dollars on a fancy, zippable, multi-colored nylon masterpiece of a playhouse for your kid. Or, you could drape an old bed sheet over a couple of chairs. Trust me: a toddler won't care about the difference. Ellie has one of the nylon contraptions above, with separate rooms to arrange and attach. It comes with mesh windows, a basketball goal and a floor covered with plastic play balls. It has bright yellow tubes to crawl through and zip-up flaps for doors. My daughter looks at it occasionally while playing with her rocks.

But a few weeks ago at Jo-Jo's house, Ellie's grandmother covered a card table with a blue bed sheet. Now all Ellie can talk about is the tent at Jo-Jo's. She wants to make one at our house—despite the expensive, commercially manufactured "tent" she already owns. Kids like the enclosure, the climbing in and out, even the solitude. So pull the kitchen chairs out from the table, take the sheets off the bed and go play.

You don't have to break the bank to give a toddler a good time. By and large, kids make their own fun. All you have to provide is a little help jump-starting the imagination. Save the money for something else—food, college, diapers. And if all else fails, go find some rocks.

MY DAUGHTER LOOKS AT IT OCCASIONALLY
WHILE PLAYING WITH HER ROCKS.

CHEAP WAYS TO SCRAPBOOK

By Margaret Feinberg

If left unchecked, scrapbooking can easily become an addiction. Millions have found fun, fellowship, and a creative outlet through this hobby. It's a great way to record memories, preserve photographs, and develop photo albums even strangers want to look through.

But anyone who has ventured into scrapbooking knows it isn't cheap. Specialty stores are brimming with gadgets of all sizes, shapes, and designs. Handmade paper, stickers designed by well-known artists, and scissors with shaped blades overflow from specially designed bins. From unique paper cutting devices to glue dispensers, the possibilities seem endless, and so does the final bill.

Yes, scrapbooking can be expensive, but here are some ways to cut back (pun intended).

GO FOR THE MASS

Because of the growing popularity of scrapbooking, mass discounters including Wal-Mart and Target are stocking scrapbook supplies. Items such as paper and glue are sold in packets rather than individually. These stores tend to stock the basics, and while the selection may not be as good as specialty stores, the prices are usually better.

For comparable or slightly higher prices and a better selection, head to retail chain craft stores such as Michael's or Hobby Lobby, which have at least half of, if not an entire aisle, dedicated to scrapbooking. In both mass discounters and retail chains, keep an eye on the aisles around the scrapbooking section. Some of the same tools used for other crafts, such as stamping, can be used for scrapbooking and can be found at lower prices.

Stationery, business supply, and paper stores are particularly helpful. They often sell large sheets of handmade and specially designed paper that can be cut up and used for scrapbooking. Be sure to ask a clerk if it's acid-free before purchasing.

Finally, make a scrapbooking specialty store your last stop. This is where you will find the one-of-a kind devices and decorations that will make your scrapbook stand out.

The same rules that apply to savvy shopping apply to scrapbooking. Make a list of what you need before you go. Establish a budget, including a little room for irresistible items. Keep an eye on the newspaper before you go, because stores will often have coupons and sales to help save you money. Also, sign up for special mailing lists from specialty stores. These will alert you to upcoming sales, coupons, and shopping opportunities.

DON'T GO ALONE

One of the biggest joys of scrapbooking is doing it in groups. Not only will scrapbooking with others help build your friendships, but it will also help lessen the financial burden. Talk to the owner of a specialty scrapbooking store to find out about any organized scrapbook events to make new friends and get new ideas. Paper cutting devices can run into the hundreds and even thousands of dollars. By sharing resources, you can save a lot of money. Consider buying bulk scrapbooking materials with a friend rather than letting the extra supplies sit unused in a drawer. When scrapbooking with friends, take advantage of access to paper punches and other cutting devices. Store the extra cuts in an envelope or plastic bag for future use.

THINK OUTSIDE THE BOX

Instead of purchasing designer scrapbook materials, create your own. Instead of using paper as a background, consider using fabric. Experiment with raffia. Walk through a local craft store with an open mind. What is something different that could be used to decorate a scrapbook? Consider using inexpensive items such as frozen treat sticks, yarn, ribbons, cotton balls, buttons, and crayons. Think about items around your house that could be used to scrapbook: used greeting cards, cartoons from the newspaper, and wrapping paper. Use acid-free index cards to frame photos. Use acid-free address labels to make notes and record specific dates, places, and memories on pages. Use chalk to write on pages. Cover photos, and spray with hairspray to preserve the chalk.

Use old children's books to create colorful photo corners and borders. Use a toenail clipper to round edges of photos and frames.

Instead of purchasing lettering, create your own by taking photos that will provide solid backgrounds. Whether it's a picture of the sky for blue, a rock for gray or the sand for white, make sure you get double prints. Then cut the letters you need out of the photos and glue into your book.

Rather than buy new markers and pens, find out if any of those you already have are acid free. Instead of buying a photo organizer use an old shoebox, plastic bags and index cards. If you make a mistake, don't forget to flip the page over, and always save your scraps for punches and future pages.

Keep an envelope with you when you take trips. Save ticket stubs, brochures, local magazines, pressed flowers, and other little items that can be used to decorate your scrapbook later on.

THINK LONG TERM ABOUT PHOTOGRAPHY

To reduce the costs of photography, consider investing in a digital camera which allows you to delete any photos you don't want, change film less often, and know when to retake a photo if one doesn't turn out. If you decide to go digital, consider investing a little extra in rechargeable batteries. It will save you in the long run.

Shop around for the best processing rates. Wal-Mart, Costco and Sam's Club offer competitive prices. Independent photo stores usually have at least one day a week where they discount prices.

If friends or children are in your photos, always order double prints. This is usually less expensive than ordering re-prints. If your photos are particularly crowded with people, shop around for a good rate on triple prints. Consider buying film in bulk with a friend. If you buy it alone, make sure it doesn't go bad.

GO ONLINE

From ideas for page layouts to chat rooms with fellow scrapbookers, a number of resources are available online for scrapbookers. Rather than buying idea books, use the information on the web. You may also find supplies at reduced costs by typing in the key words "scrapbook auction."

You can also use your computer to print out clip art and scrapbook graphic pages, and a number of websites, including *www.scrapbookscrapbook.com*, offer free samples.

DON'T GO OVERBOARD

Remember that hobbies come and go. If you fall behind in scrapbooking, don't let it overwhelm you. Simply start again. Just make sure you don't buy more supplies until you've used up the majority of what you've already purchased. And never forget that the purpose of scrapbooking is still to preserve photos. That is the focus, not the cute stickers, trendy prints, and colorful photo cards. Even though they're fun, it's far more important to invest in acid-free paper and pens that will preserve your photos for years to come.

CHEAP WAYS TO MAKE A COSTUME

By Jason Boyett

This fall, when the leaves start to turn and pumpkin patches begin to sprout from recreational vehicles in parking lots, try a little experiment. Go to a social gathering. Gather up some friends. Get their attention and say this: "Hey! We should have a costume party for Halloween!"

Here's a guarantee—half the group will respond enthusiastically. The other half will groan. Some people love the creativity and imagination that costume parties bring. Others hate having to find a last-minute outfit, pay through the roof for it, and suffer for three hours dressed as a ballerina. I know I did. But that was third grade and another story. Let's move on.

Truth is, costume parties—Halloween or otherwise—are a great opportunity for self-expression. For one evening, you can be whatever you want to be—dorky, inspired, contradictory, or any combination of the three. And you can do it without going into debt. All it takes is a little creativity and a willingness to go beyond the usual pirate/witch/vampire/princess school of costume cliché.

GO AS SOMEONE YOU KNOW

This is a great way to merge both cheapness and creativity—go as a friend. We all know someone with a unique fashion sense. Why not be that person at a party? Ask he/she if you can borrow some of their clothes. Find something—a flashy dress, his/her 1993 Aerosmith concert T-shirt, his/her favorite ratty jeans and Abercrombie hat—that your acquaintances will recognize. It's even better if your subject has a uniform or company attire from their workplace. When others ask who you're supposed to be, just grin and say, "Steve." (Unless, of course, you're not going as "Steve." Try to keep up, okay?) If needed, get one of those "Hi! My name is…" nametags and identify yourself. Trust me. People will get a kick out of it. Especially Steve.

GO AS SOMEONE NOBODY KNOWS

Same instructions as above, except easier—you don't have to borrow a friend's clothing. Just go to the thrift store and pick out an outfit. Better yet, go to the back of your closet and pick out stuff you never wear. Slap on a trusty nametag, choose a name for yourself, and walk confidently to your destination. Be prepared for the inevitable. People will look at you, eyeball your nametag, and suspiciously ask, "So who are you supposed to be?" You'll answer, pointing to your nametag with profound self-assurance: "Me? I'm Jerry. You know, Jerry?" Chances are, they won't know Jerry. You'll shrug as if it's their loss, and walk off. They'll stand there confused, trying to figure out who "Jerry" is, and you'll gain a few extra coolness points for generating mystery. Good job, Jerry.

DON'T GO, BUT SAY YOU DID

Here's the absolute easiest and cheapest costume ever, and I write that with utter conviction. It requires skill, confidence, and cunning. Also laziness. Here's the trick: Don't dress up for the costume party at all. In fact, don't even attend. The next day, when someone asks you why you weren't there, greet him or her with a blank stare. "What do you mean?" you'll reply. "I was there. You probably just didn't see me." Your fellow conversant will then inquire about your costume. This is the tricky part. You'll answer: "Oh. I went as the invisible man. Must have been a better costume than I thought."

Okay. The three previous ideas are probably a little too conceptual for most people, especially those who don't enjoy being mocked by the baseball player next to the punch bowl who spent forty-five dollars renting his cheeseball Yankees uniform and squeezing into tight pants. Loser. So for those of you who are looking for more costumey costumes, here you go:

GRAPES

Supplies: Purple balloons. Safety pins. Optional purple sweatshirt or T-shirt.

Blow up the balloons and pin them to your shirt. Wear as many as possible, cramming them as close together as you can. Top it off with a green hat of some kind, and—presto!—you're a bunch of grapes. For a variation on the theme, pin on balloons of different colors. Add a few yards of plastic cling wrap around the middle, and your costume becomes a bag of jellybeans. The fun never ends!

CRAYON

Supplies: Solid-colored sweatsuit, matching posterboard, black felt or fabric paint.

Two easy ways to do this one. First, buy a cheap sweatsuit (you can usually get one for less than ten dollars at a craft store or discount center). Using the felt, cut out shapes that match the black ink on Crayola crayons, then glue them to the sweatshirt with fabric glue (You can also paint it on with fabric paint, but this may prevent you from using the shirt later—unless you have no qualms about wearing a crayon shirt, just for kicks). The felt will adhere to the fabric with the glue, but can be removed later. Finally, cut a cone-shaped hat out of the posterboard. Tie an elastic chinstrap to it, pull it on, and you're a crayon.

Idea #2: Forego all the preparation, supplies, and specifications. Instead, just wear a sweatsuit in your favorite solid color. Tell people "I'm the color yellow." Find six friends to do the same thing with other colors and you can arrive collectively as a rainbow. Or as the color wheel. Or as soldiers from the board game Risk.

ALPHABET

Supplies: White sweatsuit, or jeans with white T-shirt. Black fabric paint or felt.

Paint or apply a huge black letter to your chest (just pick a favorite). Your costume? A letter of the alphabet. Add extra touches to make it even more unique. Blacken one eye, put a "P" on your chest, and you're a black-eyed pea. Or, become the letter "M." Get a friend to dress just like you, and arrive together. The two of you are an "M&M" or "Eminem." Combine an "N," a "B" and a "C," and you're network television. Find two friends who'll wear a "W" to match yours, and the three of you can be the Internet. Oh, the possibilities ...

LAUNDRY

Supplies: Various items of laundry, safety pins, optional laundry basket.

Wear something solid like an all-black outfit, then pin small laundry items (socks, underwear, panty hose, sheets of fabric softener) to it. You're static cling. Or, do the same thing, but add a laundry basket to the mix. Buy a cheap one at the discount store and cut a hole in the bottom of it. Make the hole big enough to slide over your head and shoulders, but small enough to rest on your hips. Fill the basket with laundry, then pin additional items onto your shirt. Congratulations: You're laundry.

BOXES

Find a big box. Your best bet is to procure one of the boxes computer companies use to ship monitors or systems—you'll want something at least twenty-four inches across and pretty close to square. Cut two leg holes in the bottom, an armhole in each side, and a large hole at the top for your head (and for costume entry).

Least creative idea: Stop right there. Don't decorate any further. Just be a box, a simple, humble, no-nonsense box. Woo hoo.

More creative idea: Spray paint the box white, then affix or paint large black circles on each side to turn it into a single dice. Or more appropriately, a die. With this costume, it's preferable to go along with a partner. That way, you can say, "We're a pair of dice." If you go alone, you'll have to keep saying, "Hi! I'm a die!" People might get the wrong idea, and take it as either a threat of violence or a suicidal cry for help. If you start getting head-tilting questions like, "Hey, how have things been going for you? Feeling okay?" then clear up the misunderstanding ASAP. No sense ruining a good party.

Most creative idea: Cut out nine squares each of red, orange, yellow, blue, green, and white construction paper. Draw a grid and glue the squares on the box in random order. Fondly recall the eighties: You're a Rubik's Cube.

Cheap, creative costumes require little more than a couple bucks, a little resourcefulness, and a willingness to look like, well, laundry for a few hours. Or a crayon. How hard can that be? Get started, and be careful with the safety pins.

CHEAP WAYS TO CARPE DIEM
BY MARGARET FEINBERG

Every so often you need to take time for yourself. It's easy to skip, especially with the demands of just plain old living life, whether it's raising children, maintaining a marriage, or contributing in the workplace. Yet taking time off—whether it's a few hours, a full day, or an entire weekend—can help transform your attitude, appearance, and ability to serve and love those around you.

Fortunately, having a great day doesn't require making or spending lots of money. It simply takes an upgrade in attitude, a pinch of appreciation, and a portion of creativity. Here are a few ways to carpe your diem:

TAKE CARE OF YOUR BODY

Enjoy an outdoor activity. Give yourself a facial. Take a bubble bath. Eat a meal consisting of just fruits and vegetables. Go on a long walk. Stop to enjoy the views and people you encounter. Make a smoothie. Spend some time on your nails. Don't set the alarm one morning. Take your dog for a walk. If you don't have one, take someone else's. Skip the soda and coffee. Drink eight glasses of water. Hop in a hot tub.

Wash your hair and use extra conditioner. Play a sport. Join the gym. Take a nap. Learn how to belly dance. Give yourself a mud mask. Floss. Buy new pajamas. Get a massage. Go swimming. Take vitamin supplements. Buy a new pair of shoes. Start an exercise program. Pick up a new sport. Take a stroll after dinner with a loved one. Hang your feet in a stream or pond.

CARDF

DIEM

TAKE CARE OF YOUR SOUL

Wake up early and watch the sunrise. Sit outside and enjoy the sunset. Look for ways to make the simple things in life extraordinary. Use cloth napkins instead of paper. Choose to eat outside instead of in. Place fresh flowers by your bed. Go to church. Volunteer. Drink orange juice in the mornings from a wineglass. Practice random acts of kindness. Spend a day working with the poor.

Pick wildflowers and create a colorful, fragrant bouquet. Plan a vacation. Make a dream to-do list. Have lunch at an outdoor cafe. Go out to a nice restaurant for just dessert and coffee. Plant something wonderful in your garden. If you don't have a garden, buy a large pot and plant fresh flowers or spices and tend them. Visit the library and check out a best-selling book. Spend the day reading it. Go fishing. Forgive.

Go to an airport simply to watch people. Read a chapter or two of the Bible. Pray. Enjoy a hot cup of tea. Listen to your favorite song over and over again. Make a list of all the things you're thankful for. Enjoy a slushee.

TAKE CARE OF YOUR RELATIONSHIPS

Organize a picnic. Go online and track down old friends. Call or email them. Hold hands with someone you love. Bake cookies and give them away. Go the extra mile for a customer or someone you work with. Give a gift to someone for no reason. Write personal notes to at least three people in your life who have been faithful friends. Try to say "thank you" at least a dozen times today. Send twenty dollars to someone who really needs it.

Travel to a nearby town or city and spend the day hanging out with a pal. Go through your old emails and send an update to people you've lost touch with. Write thank you notes to five people you work with who are under-appreciated. Create your own day spa with some friends. Give someone a good hug.

Go through old stacks of photos and send some of those no one has ever seen to friends. Grab a camera, film, and friend and create your own photo shoot. Make a home video. Make new memories.

Apologize to a friend or loved one. Ask for forgiveness. Then, make up.

TAKE CARE OF YOUR SMILE

Enter a competition and don't worry about your time or rank. Enjoy the experience. Laugh. Make time to journal. Go dancing. Talk to your mom. Or dad. Or grandma. Or grandpa. Or sibling. Or other family member you dearly love. Create something out of papier-mâché. Eat ice cream right out of the carton. Dance alone in the living room. Watch a television show that makes you laugh. Read a joke book. Reflect on favorite moments in your life. Visit a petting zoo. Hold and touch the softest animals.

Hold your own "Me Day" in which you pamper yourself with everything you love. Wear your favorite outfit, eat your favorite foods, watch your favorite movies, and do something special just for you. For an even better experience, hold a Me Day with someone else, where you both make a list of your favorite things and do them together.

CREATE SOMETHING OUT OF PAPIER-MÂCHÉ.
EAT ICE CREAM RIGHT OUT OF THE CARTON.
DANCE ALONE IN THE LIVING ROOM.
WATCH A TELEVISION SHOW THAT MAKES YOU LAUGH.
READ A JOKE BOOK.
REFLECT ON FAVORITE MOMENTS IN YOUR LIFE.
VISIT A PETTING ZOO.
HOLD AND TOUCH THE SOFTEST ANIMALS.

CHEAP WAYS TO BUY ART SUPPLIES

By Katie Meier

Fuzzy pipe cleaners, you might recall, are the rare and refined devices used with painted egg cartons through which third-grade-style tarantulas seem to materialize out of thin air. Though art itself knows no bounds, art supplies surely should.

Getting art supplies cheaply has everything to do with understanding the differences, similarities, and disparities between the terms "art," "craft," and "hardware." While supplies from each realm might cross in and out with regard to the type of art that's made, the cost of these supplies differs significantly depending on what classification—and thus what store you choose to do your shopping in.

ART

The technical definition for art waxes with words like "conscious production," "works of beauty," and "quality of conception or execution." But for anyone who's been to the local Modern Museum of Art lately, thems' fightin' words, as art now includes Lego-made crucifixes featuring Spiderman and animals on the half-sheet enclosed only by plastic and preservative liquid. So, it goes without saying that nearly anything fits these days in terms of art. Rather than fight over what should be included, better to battle over what it should cost to create; the difference lies in who is selling.

Those stores that advertise "art" in their title aren't necessary the only, or cheapest, vendors of art supplies. Art-marts that masquerade as art-only, or art-centric shops are prime places to avoid if you're looking for deals. Ask yourself why a store claiming to specialize in art also features sections like "Furniture and Function?" Count on the high cost of maintaining such store diversity to be passed on in the price of every pencil and every gallon of primer you purchase.

Get yourself into a specialized store for the best rates. Stores that stock the particulars order bigger, have more left over, and thus bring prices down in the already escalated world of art-supply inflation. In addition, artists are notoriously fickle. Not surprisingly, so are the makers of their supplies. Look for discontinued styles, items, sizes, or shapes to save big.

Also, consider what materials make up the items you'd like to buy. For example, a prepared canvas consists of the following: canvas, primer, nails/staples, and stretcher bars. With this deconstruction done it becomes obvious whether we can build an item cheaper by getting to the basics. Canvas can be bought at a fabric store; nails/staples can be shot through a gun available for purchase at any hardware store, as is the wood required to make the stretcher bars. It might take more work and a little research, but hey…nobody ever said cheap meant easy.

CRAFT

The word "crafty" is now a socially appropriate adjective used in a sort of complex symbolic crafter system. "She's *totally* crafty" is really the signal to the decoupage-disabled: "She knows how to smear clear glaze over collected post-cards and is thus, decidedly cool." But cool connotations aside, the real question to ask crafters is what kind of costs they're paying to create "shabby-chic" and other looks all across the land.

Many "craft" stores sell exactly what they should: items used to construct. From thread and fabric to floral oasis and stencil templates, craft stores should specialize in the items necessary to assemble. However, those items that follow assembly—say, the paint, glaze, glitter, or other accompaniments to constructed items—should be bought elsewhere, as these items are as generic as Dr. Skipper and other well known knock-offs despite the attempt by stores to repackage and re-price products for the "craft" crowd. There's no sense in buying "Country Crafter Silly Sand Paper: Fine Grain" for five dollars per pop when every woodworker knows you can by it for pennies a sheet at a hardware store. Even scarier is the selection craft stores purport as "art supply." Crayola isn't king. Watch out for one broadly marketed brand-name vendor, as price gauging can't be too far behind such limited set-ups.

HARDWARE

The real beauty behind Mega-Home and those super-multi-monstrous outlet stores is how many supplies they sell for the artist. Of course, to get it cheap you'll have to learn to speak a new language: blue-collar banter, we'll call it. Handy-people have known this stuff for years, replacing pricey packaged items with brown-bag alternatives.

For example, say "paint palette" (twenty dollars) in art-speak becomes "Lexan-Plexiglas" squares (two dollars) in blue-collar banter. I'm sorry, did you say "Testrite studio reflector and light ($16.95 + 9.45)?" I think you meant "standard clamp light and shade" ($7.95), didn't you? And while language overlap will apply in some places—an apron is an apron, you know?—the hardware crowd has less interest in pricey aesthetic versions of handy-dandy items like rulers, T-squares, rolls of tape, work clamps, tool boxes, and other art supply supplements.

In addition to deciphering the difference between "art," "craft," and "hardware," know the difference between impulse buying and ordering for the long haul. The cheapest art supplies are those you'll actually use, so be specific when you enter the store, as appropriately placed point-of-purchase (POP) displays can lure your money away. POPs are the infamous by-the-register gizmos and doo-dads that shine with such speculative luster they simply can't be done without. But as the item is likely to lie under your bed next to the Ab-Flex you were speculating about as well, better to skip it and decrease the total cost of the day's purchases.

And last, for needs that are long term, like canvas, paper, or pencils, get to the online site of your favorite art supplier. There, deals abound and can be had in bulk: Go for it—you'll get to the last of that 220 pack of pencils eventually.

CHEAP WAYS TO THROW A BBQ
By Margaret Feinberg

The good news is that you don't have to be Martha Stewart to throw a great barbecue. All you need is a little planning, some creativity, and guests.

LOCATION, LOCATION, LOCATION

It's generally easiest to throw a barbecue in your own home, where you know where everything is and have access to every item. If your home is not big enough, is being remodeled or is not in an ideal location, ask a friend if you can throw the event at their house. Or consider organizing one at a nearby park, lake, or beach.

CHARCOAL VS. GAS

The benefits and cost effectiveness of charcoal versus gas grills have long been debated. Low-end charcoal grills are priced at half or more less than a low-end gas grill. They are fairly easy to assemble and provide a genuine charcoal taste. They also take at least a half-hour to heat up and require repeatedly buying bags of charcoal.

Gas grills provide instant heat, and gas canisters only need to be refilled every six months or so depending on use. The food still gets the grilled flavor, though charcoal fans will testify that it's not quite as good.

If you're strapped for cash or on a budget, go for the charcoal grill. If you have a little extra to spend or are willing to shop at a garage sale to pick one up (moving sales are ideal), then a gas grill is worth the investment. All grills, and especially floor models, can be found on sale at the end of the summer. Try to buy a floor model that is already assembled or purchase it from a store that will put it together for you. The process takes an afternoon, and there are usually mysterious pieces left over.

BULKING UP

As with any grocery list, it's best to buy food in bulk. Discount warehouse stores such as Sam's Club and Costco are great places to stock up on popular items. But keep an eye on local grocery store sales, too. Their promotional items can prove to cost less than the mass discounters.

This is particularly true for meat. Take advantage of any buy-one-get-one-free sales at the local supermarket. Stock up your freezer. Always marinate whatever you buy to give it a distinct flavor.

If you plan on throwing a few events during the summer, buy key items when they're on sale. Grocery stores tend to offer their best sales around holiday weekends such as Memorial Day, Fourth of July and Labor Day. Stock up on sodas, meats, and barbecue sauces then.

Buy items that offer a lot of bang for your buck. Invest in large bags of chips, watermelons, and other food items that can be shared among crowds. Try to buy seasonal fruits and vegetables. Avoid foods that tend to go bad quickly, melt, or have offensive odors. A summer barbecue probably isn't the time to pick up an ice cream cake or create your favorite tuna fish salad. Ranch rolls are great for a barbecue. They're inexpensive and can be used as bread for sandwiches or warmed and served with butter.

Don't be afraid to ask your friends and family members to bring something with them. Whether it's drinks, a bag of chips, or a side dish, most people are more than willing to contribute. If you already have everything you need, you might mention that you'll need a hand cleaning up afterward.

When possible, create side dishes from scratch rather than buying them in bulk. It's far less expensive to make a potato salad than to buy it from the deli. Most all-American side dishes such as pasta salad are inexpensive to make. Call your mom or neighbor for recipes.

Remember to keep it simple. You don't need to offer two dozen sides or six different types of beverages. Offer the basics. Bring along sealable plastic bags so food doesn't go to waste. Send people home with the extras or bundle them up for the freezer or refrigerator.

PLAYTIME

Create activities for the barbecue. People will remember having a good time more than having good food. Organize games for kids and adults—a game of volleyball, swimming, or even a board game. Keep a football, deck of cards, and other equipment around for guests to enjoy. Bring a radio or CD player for music and to add atmosphere to the event. And buy a bottle or two of bug spray in case people stay late into the afternoon or evening.

GET CREATIVE

What can you do to make your event a little different or more enjoyable? Consider buying western handkerchiefs on sale and have guests use them as napkins. Invite them to keep them as party favors. You'll be surprised how many guests wear them after they've eaten. Consider serving beverages in mason jars.

Hide a coin, covered in plastic, in a cake or desert. Give whoever discovers it a prize. Hand out plastic sheriff's badges to any children who attend. Buy or make your own piñata.

Pick out some simple, inexpensive decorations. Do you have an American flag you can use as a backdrop? Balloons can be blown up to add a festive touch. If you have access to wildflowers, pick them and create small bouquets.

If you're using any particularly popular recipes that you know guests will love, print a few copies out on the computer before the event. Then, when admirers ask for the recipe, you'll be ready!

CHEAP WAYS TO ENTERTAIN YOURSELF WITH MEDIA By Josh Hatcher

We all have this insatiable urge for entertainment. We have hundreds of CDs, videos, and DVDs. People fork over billions of dollars to entertain themselves. Movie stars, authors, athletes, and musicians live high off the hog—high off of your hog, to be precise. Here are some ways you can keep yourself entertained, but not ship all your money directly to the pockets of the "Rich and Famous."

THE DOLLAR THEATER

They are out there, especially in college towns. It's the Wal-Mart of the cinema. Tons of movies, a couple months later than they premiered, for a buck fifty. Most theaters charge seven or eight dollars. Hey, I would rather see a movie a few months later if it means jingle in my own pocket. They typically make their money on overpriced popcorn and soda, so eat and drink before you go, or sneak in a bag of snacks in your date's handbag. You may not be able to discuss the latest film releases as soon as they hit the theatre, but with the money you'll save, you could see three times as many flicks!

THE LIBRARY

Don't knock it. Libraries are not just for smelly old ladies! They often have videos and DVDs for loan. That means they're free. Instead of $2.50 a night, all you need is a library card and money for a late fee if you forget to bring it back. You can also borrow books for free, surf the net, read magazines, and some of them even have toys. What do you have to lose?

JOIN THE CLUB

You've all got those special offers in your mailbox: DVDs for ninety-nine cents, twelve CDs for the price of one, four free books if you buy two. Consider actually joining. If you make sure to send those annoying cards back, and if you only pay full price for the commitment purchase, you can save hundreds of dollars on trips to the record shop or the bookstore. Every few months these companies give specials and incentives, and you can get your items for as cheap as 80 percent off. If you have the organizational skills, and the patience to wait for the really good deals, it's for you.

THE INTERNET

While days can be spent on the ethics of file-sharing, the fact still remains that thousands of CDs, movies, computer games, and more are available for download. Depending on your ethical standpoint, you can download from any given media at any given time. For those a bit squeamish about peer-to-peer applications, there are tons of streaming Internet radio stations, television stations, and downloadable mp3s from artists who don't mind sharing their work with you for free.

SECOND HAND

Instead of forking over twenty bucks at the record shop for that rare U2 album that reminds you of your first car, get it used. Check out the pawn shops in town, hang out at yard sales, and become an eBay expert. Someone is bound to have purchased it and not had that burning passion to keep it. If the CD you are purchasing is scratched, you can invest in a scratch repair kit, and it can restore CDs to their original condition, so it will be like new.

SELL IT

If you have CDs or videos that you have listened to once, and determined that it wasn't your cup of tea, or even listened to a hundred times, but no longer desire, sell them. Maybe your tastes have changed from Paula Abdul to Enya. Someone somewhere out there is just crazy about Paula Abdul, and willing to shell out some cold hard cash that you could use to satisfy your Enya craving. You can sell via eBay, the used music section at your record store, or anywhere else that you have seen used CDs being traded.

STREET TEAMS

If there are artists or labels that you really dig and want to support, many of them have street teams. Applicants from across the country sign up to receive free CDs, stickers, and videos by helping promote them. It's for those who have a knack for telling friends about music or hanging up flyers around college.

WRITE REVIEWS

Put up a website or hook up with an online magazine, and let them know that you are interested in reviewing new music. Record companies and film companies send out prereleases and host press screenings to be reviewed constantly. If you have a bit of writing talent, it's worth utilizing it to get free CDs or free movie tickets.

GAMING

Each year Sega, Sony, Nintendo, Microsoft, and the rest of the gaming industry try to market new gaming systems. People pay thousands of dollars to be the first to get one. But every time a new system comes out, the price of the last system falls ridiculously low. So why not wait a year to buy the previously popular gaming system? Buying new games can cost forty to one hundred dollars per game, and if you get a game you don't like, you might as well kiss your cash goodbye. Try renting the game from the local video store for a night. If the graphics rock and you really like it, check eBay to see if someone else is parting with it for less than the retail price.

CHEAP WAYS TO HOST A RETREAT

By Margaret Feinberg

Hosting a retreat, whether it's for friends, family, or a church group, can be fun and rewarding. By their nature, retreats tend to be low in cost because you're able to buy everything in bulk—from reservations to activities to food.

A LITTLE PLANNING GOES A LONG WAY

The first thing you need to determine is how many people you expect to attend your retreat. Depending on the numbers, you may have to reserve a large or a small facility. Talk to potential attendees. If possible, get a definite list of yeas and nays. Begin promoting several months in advance. Ask for non-refundable deposits to confirm spots. People are less likely to cancel once they've invested their own money.

Once you know your numbers and have determined the time of year for the event, begin exploring options. Don't limit yourself to your hometown. Explore nearby cities and even far away resorts. Try to think of places that would be considered off-season. If you're looking for a bargain for a summer event, try calling ski resorts. If you're looking for one during the winter, try beach resort towns. You can save a bundle by booking in the off season.

Once you've determined the place, begin calling around. Contact the local chamber of commerce for a listing of facilities that will accommodate your group. Try to negotiate prices with the hotel manager, who will be most likely to have the authority to offer steep discounts. Look for off-the-beaten-path retreat centers, including churches and monasteries that provide a quiet setting. Camps and YMCAs can offer low cost alternatives during the busy summer months. College dorms are another alternative during the summer term when students are away. Whatever location you decide upon, make sure it appeals to the majority of your attendees. If the place is below their personal standards or above their price range, you're going to lose attendees.

Talk to others who have organized a similar event. What facilities did they use? What were the strengths and weaknesses of each facility? If possible, visit the site you choose before booking it.

Keep in mind the amenities available at each site. How large are the meeting rooms? Is there an additional cost to use them? Is there a swimming pool or hot tub? Is shopping close by?

Find out when final deposits are due, if there is any negotiation in the final head count, and what the damage deposit requirements are. Generally it's a good idea to underestimate attendance if a large financial commitment is involved and overestimate if attendance costs are low or even free. Don't pick your final number out of the air. Base it on previous retreats or outreaches and be realistic. If you're concerned that the final price will make it impossible for a handful of people to attend, consider raising the overall price by a few dollars and adding partial or full scholarships.

Read all the print in the contract and know the cancellation policy.

FEEDING THE CROWD

Will the establishment provide food? If so, which meals are the most expensive? Could you provide any of them as part of the retreat and save attendees money? Breakfast is generally an easy one. A few dozen bagels with cream cheese, donuts and a few gallons of orange juice can go a long way. Throw in some fresh fruit such as bananas and apples and you'll have some happy campers.

If some of the meals are too expensive, consider allowing attendees to be responsible for one or more of their own meals. Before you do, make sure there are suitable and easily accessible restaurants in the immediate area.

Make sure that any meals not covered in the registration are clearly noted in the promotional material so there aren't any surprises for guests. Communicate with the facility to confirm which meals they are responsible for providing.

SPEAKING UP

Finding a speaker on a particular topic can be extremely expensive. It will usually require paying all travel expenses as well as a fee. Research lesser-known speakers. You can do this by finding books written on the topic you want addressed and contacting the authors directly. Ask family and friends to recommend people they know who would be knowledgeable. Always check references on the speaker selected and ask to preview a video or tape if possible.

Make sure the retreat center can supply equipment for the speaker. Is there a sound system? Television? VCR? Display for a power point presentation? And will you have to pay extra for these services? If so, don't forget to include them in the registration costs.

DON'T GO IT ALONE

Organizing a retreat and making sure it runs smoothly can be exhausting. Solicit help from attendees. Most people are more than willing to give you a hand cleaning up, carrying items, or distributing literature. Afterward, acknowledge their efforts with a card or small gift.

TREATS

Retreat guests love freebies. If you're organizing a large event with a focused topic, try to get sponsors. Companies will often provide free literature, books, products, and gifts to attendees if they're part of their target market. It's worth calling companies to ask.

For most guests, there's nothing like the surprise of finding something awaiting them in their room. A bottle of lotion with a ribbon around it, a small bag of chocolates, or a scented candle with a note can do wonders in making your guests feel welcome.

CHEAP WAYS TO GIFT WRAP
By Katie Meier

With a water hose unraveling neatly out of her fabulously old-school farm bin, my aunt sprinkles a shower of droplets over her luscious garden, grown out across the edges of her perfectly worn brick walkway; tea-lights twinkle with the beads of water that reach them as they wait to be lit at night; lanterns nestled softly amidst the many flowers sway with the weight of the water as it trickles on, and then off, the sides. And at that very moment I realize she really isn't like Martha, no matter what her neighbors say; she's even better ... she's lives a little lower down the income line and is a middle class whiz at making low cost living—and giving—look like a million bucks. From her table to yours, here are her best tips for learning to gift-wrap like the pros.

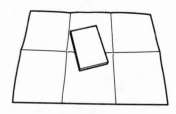

STOCK PILE

Low cost wrapping begins with lots of storage space. The reason? Prices for the particulars of wrapping vary from season to season. To get the best deals, you'll need to stock up after the season's gone. Sure you'll look silly buying for Christmas at Easter, but who cares? Buy all you can to save big and store it away for use throughout the year.

THE ICING IS THE BEST PART

Wire is the only way to go with wrapping if you're looking to make ribbon the focal point of a package. Because wire ribbon can cost you, it's best to buy it on sale. Not all ribbon is seasonal, but what's not is still affected by style, sending a predictable percentage to the bargain bin over time. But be sure to keep and eye on where you're shopping; chic card or gift stores can't rival the ribbon discounts you'll find at fabric, craft, or even online stores—like paper or wrapping sites—that stock ribbon as a significant part of their inventory. Also, wire-rimmed ribbon can usually be found making an infamous fifty-pack appearance at your local warehouse-superstore during the holiday seasons. These packaged deals can be a steal if you buy in bulk. In addition, wire ribbon can be made if you're abundantly crafty and have no aversion to getting down to business with a glue gun. Simply run a thin rope of wire on the inside edges of a length of ribbon, then flip the edge in and seal it snug with a thin bead of glue.

RAFFIA

Learn the word "raffia" well. Technically the term refers to "an African palm tree having large leaves that yield a useful fiber." But here were talking about the dried strands of good old *Raphia ruffia* that make each and every package look great. If you don't have a visual on what exactly raffia is, it's the thin brown tie that seems to accompany every "Uber-Eco-Friendly" product on the market. Raffia can be bunched together and tied to make flowers seem fresh from the country, or it can be used to make bows for cellophane wrapped baskets to give that natural glow. All this glamour can be yours by the four-dollar bag.

KRAFT IS KING

Kraft isn't just for kids, or for macaroni. Kraft paper is king when it comes to simple, cost effective wrapping and bests the price for those busy, printed, and patterned papers by a mile. While regular wrapping paper can cost nearly five dollars a roll for just a few feet, kraft bought in bulk will give you these few feet plus about one thousand more for around ten bucks. Beyond price, brown rolls beat out all else as they let creativity rule, offering a blank slate for each gift occasion; from decorative designs on top to cutting and pasting a creative gift bag, brown kraft is cheap not only because of its price but because of its mutability. Rolls of the wrap can be purchased at any paper or school supply store, and can often be found in a few other colors.

GET PERSONAL

Move photography out of the frame. Wrapping great gifts has everything to do with being unique, and photographs allow a personalized package for pennies. To make each parcel person-worthy, take any photograph and have it enlarged on paper. This process costs nearly nothing at the local Quick-Copy-It-Fast-Mart, where there is even a choice of paper types and colors for those who pay a bit more. Add colored pencils to make the gift complete, giving portraits and landscapes colors never imagined before your one-of-a-kind wrapping.

LET IT SHINE

Let the outside shine. Gift-wrap greats are well known for their ability to unite disparate items into a seemingly beautiful mix. Take those sausage company baskets for instance; who knew that salami, some jam, and a jar of barbeque sauce could look so great together? Even those who don't like the theme of the basket have been known to poke their noses around this kind of gift, just to see what might be lurking within the outer wrap. You can create this same mystique if you learn to love cellophane. The cheap, clear substance holds all manner of items together in unity, and under a high gloss shine. Like all products sold on a roll, buying bulk will cost you less.

GET GUTSY

What's on the inside counts as well, and packaging doesn't have to mean foam peanuts. With gifts, the greatest know that a package should be special all the way through. So, to get creative for less, try the following suggestion: paper grocery bags. Cut into thin strips and tossed to form a soft bed, these bags transform a plain old box into a beautiful base for your gift. The bags are thick, and dense, filling extra space in the box and keeping the gift item(s) safe. The look of the bags keeps the wrapping on the classy side as well, with the natural tone of the paper playing second fiddle to the main gift item to be wrapped.

CHEAP WAYS TO ENTERTAIN YOUR FRIENDS By Jason Boyett

Let's make one thing clear from the beginning. When the Home & Garden set speaks of "entertaining," they are referring to the process of planning, preparing, and hosting a fabulous dinner party. They concentrate on things like centerpieces and Lenox patterns and crystal stemware and delicious fondue. Much attention is paid to pine sprig napkin rings and rosemary eggplant dip and grilled asparagus.

These "entertainers" are probably not the audience of this book. And furthermore, rosemary eggplant dip is not something you want to do cheaply, at least not without unfortunate results. Therefore, scrap that definition of "entertaining" for now.

For our purposes, to entertain your friends is to show them a good time. To do it cheaply is to show them a good time without having to go out to dinner or pay for concert tickets. Entertaining your friends cheaply involves inviting people over to your home and making sure they have fun—at no cost to you. The best way to do it? Two words: party games.

Here are some cheap party games that are certain to amuse even the dullest of guests. Few preparations are needed (except for the cotton ball game), and the more players the better.

THE QUESTION GAME

How is this game played? Exactly.

Gather all players into a circle. Make sure everyone is positioned so they can turn to face the players to their immediate left and right.

How it's played: Choose a starting player. The first player (Player 1) turns to his right and asks the person next to him (Player 2) a question—any question. Player 2 *does not answer* the question she was just asked. Instead, she turns to the player to her right (Player 3) and asks a different question. The questioners must look directly into the eyes of the person they're asking.

The object of the game is to not get "out." A player is out if they do any of the following:

1) Answer the question asked of them—
even if it's in the form of another question.
2) Laugh, giggle, snort, or fail in any way to maintain complete seriousness.
3) Fail to immediately continue the rapid-fire chain of questioning.
4) Make a statement instead of a question.
5) Repeat a question asked previously in the game.

Other rules: When you're "out," you are removed from the circle. The last two remaining players ask questions back and forth of each other. There is no minimum or maximum length for questions.

Sample play:

Player 1 to Player 2: "What is the average rainfall of the Amazon basin?"
Player 2 to Player 3: "What time were you born?"
Player 3 to Player 4: "Does this look infected?"
Player 4: "Bwa-hahahahaha!" (Player 4 is out.)

Once you get the hang of it, add this fun variation to the mix: Instead of kicking a player out when she breaks the rules, make her answer the question truthfully.

COTTON BALL TRANSFER

Gather two large pots, bowls, or buckets and a bag of cotton balls. You'll also need two chairs, a big serving spoon or ladle, a blindfold, and a stopwatch.

Set up the chairs facing the same direction and at least five feet apart, with a pot or bowl on each chair. Fill the first pot with the cotton balls.

How it's played: Blindfold your first contestant. Disorient him by spinning him

HOW IS THIS GAME PLAYED? EXACTLY.

around a few times. Give him the spoon, and face him toward the cotton ball pot, which should be just a couple of feet away. Start the timer. The contestant will have sixty seconds to blindly transfer as many cotton balls as possible from one container to the other, using only the spoon. The contestant's free hand is not to be used. Only balls that actually make it into the second pot should be counted. Keep a final score for each contestant.

Why it's fun: Have you ever tried to scoop anything you can't see or feel? Not only is it inscrutably Zen-like, it's pretty stinking hard. Hilarity ensues when the first contestant carefully transfers the phantom contents of an empty spoon from one bucket to the next, thinking he's moving a load of cotton balls. You'll soon discover the vital role mockery plays in this game.

PHOTOGRAPHER

Use a point-and-shoot camera with a flash and an automatic self-timer. Gather your friends into a circle.

How it's played: Set the automatic timer on the camera, then start passing it around the circle. Each person must take the camera, point it towards themselves at arm's length (however briefly), then pass it on to the person on their right. Keep playing, pointing, and passing until the timer goes off and the camera flashes. Whoever is holding the camera when it goes off is "out." Laugh heartily, play until a single winner remains, then develop the film. Laugh some more.

A fun variation is to play in a dark or slightly dimmed room, where the camera flash will further disorient the frantic participants. If you want your camera to survive for more than one game, lay down some ground rules—hand-to-hand passing only, no throwing, no dropping.

STATING THE OBVIOUS

For a group of party guests who are unfamiliar with each other, "Stating the Obvious" is a great icebreaker game. Gather everyone into a circle.

How it's played: Choose an opening player. That player must stand in the middle of the circle, and submit to three rounds of "observations." In order, everyone in the circle gets to make a statement about the person in the center.

Round 1: Each player makes a statement starting with "It's obvious that…" The sentence must end with something verifiable, such as, "It's obvious that you have a goatee." The participant in the center cannot respond.

Round 2: Each person makes an observation starting with "I assume that…" The completed sentence must be linked to an observable fact. For example, "Since you're sporting a goatee, I assume you consider yourself relatively hip." Again, the participant is not allowed to respond.

Round 3: Each person begins "I imagine you…" Based on previous observations, the outside players can form outrageous speculations about the participant, such as, "Because of your stylish goatee, I imagine you are a sensitive musician type who lives in despair because no one understands his art." The participant, at this point, can answer true or false.

Take turns being the one on the hot seat. You'll enjoy hearing how you're perceived. And from the standpoint of the players in the circle, it's fun to see just how intuitive we can be about people we don't know. By the end of the game, everyone will have learned something interesting about one another.

From "Six Degrees of Kevin Bacon" to "Spin the Bottle," party games have long been deeply ingrained into our culture—much longer than Martha Stewart and her brand of elaborately swanky entertaining. With that in mind, let's reclaim the party game for what it is: a cheap diversion that allows us to publicly act foolish, squeal with laughter, and pose silly questions, all in the name of good fun. Go play.

CHEAP WAYS TO TAKE A SKI VACATION

BY MARGARET FEINBERG

Taking a ski vacation doesn't have to cost an arm and a leg literally or figuratively.

SKIP THE HOLIDAYS

The first step in making a ski adventure a little lighter on your pocketbook is in your selection of dates. The lift ticket prices of most major ski areas fluctuate throughout the ski season. The highest prices revolve around holidays, including Martin Luther King Day, Presidents' Day, and St. Patrick's Day, with Christmas being the most expensive of them all. The rates usually increase for the weekend or entire week around any given holiday. Check with individual resorts for a price listing.

Lift tickets aren't the only rates to go up. Lodging takes a jump, too. Rates for a rental home the week after Christmas can be as much as four times the rate of the low season. It's the most highly desired time to take a ski vacation, and those who do so pay dearly. Ironically, it's also the busiest time, lending itself to crowding on and off the slopes of resort towns. And even in Colorado, the snow can arrive late, leaving those booked with a holiday vacation with uncertain ski conditions.

For the budget-minded traveler, the best time to take a ski vacation is either the first or last two weeks of the ski year. Both contain an element of uncertainty if you're booking ahead, but the snow generally tends to be better toward the end of the season. The ski mountain has been given an opportunity to build up a base, and most ski resorts in the West receive a handful of late season snowfalls.

You can expect icy conditions in the morning and slushy conditions in the afternoon, but along with them you'll find great weather and lodging and ski ticket prices reduced 40 to 60 percent. In addition, ski shops will mark down their inventory 30 to 50 percent at the end of the season to make room for next year's arrivals. So if you're looking for a new outfit or pair of skis, it's a great time to buy. Plus, most ski towns celebrate the end of the year with specials for locals, such as two-for-one dinners (which tourists can also enjoy) at various eateries. Check the local paper upon arrival for special deals. Considering all the savings, what's a little slush?

If you're looking for optimal snow conditions for reasonable prices, head to the mountains in the second half of January. It's one of the slower times of the winter because most parents aren't willing to pull their children out of school, yet it usually promises some of the best snowfall of the season.

OFF THE BEATEN PATH

Smaller, off-the-beaten-path resorts generally have lower prices. If you're all about saving money, find a ski resort that you've never heard of and go there. Just remember that you often get what you pay for.

MULTI-DAY SKI DEALS

Most ski areas offer multiple-day lift tickets. The more days you buy the more savings you incur, but pay attention to how many dollars you're actually putting away. Often it only averages out to two to five dollars a day. If you're on a five-day ski vacation, consider buying a four or five day ticket and take a day off. That may be blasphemy in some hard core ski circles, but a day off the mountain might be the best thing for your vacation. You can engage in other activities—from shopping to dog sledding to snowmobiling—or just enjoy a day on the couch in front of the fireplace with your honey muffin and rest. Remember that it's usually easier to add on a day of skiing than to try to argue for a refund for a day you didn't use.

LODGING DEALS

If possible, take your ski vacation with another couple or group of friends in order to save on lodging. Renting a small house usually provides more square footage and comfort than a hotel room. It also guarantees a kitchen, which can save significantly on your food bill. Even if you rent a place without a kitchen, make an effort to pack your own lunches. Use the savings on a nice dinner in town.

Don't fall for all the claims of ski-in, ski-out lodging. Often it can become ski-in and hike-out or vice versa. If you're considering one of these locations, ask the booking agent if you have to hike in either direction. How far do you have to walk? How steep is the hill? Is it to your ability level? And finally, what time of the year does the snow begin to melt, creating a mud-in, mud-out experience? Ski-in, ski-out locations are usually more expensive and, depending on their exact location, can become a hassle. Consider looking for alternative lodging at a place located near the ski mountain that offers shuttle service. The majority of them do. Will the shuttle take you to other places in town, including the grocery store and restaurants? Do they offer airport pick up? If so, it can save you from having to rent a car. Find out how often the shuttle runs before making your final decision.

SPECIAL PROGRAMS

Before you book, visit the websites of the ski resorts you're considering. Sign up for any e-saver lists. Check out the policies and promotions of individual resorts. For example, Steamboat's Kids Ski Free program enables children twelve years of age or younger to ski free the same number of days as their parents when parents purchase a lift tickets for five days or more. The offer is on a one-on-one basis only, with one free child per paid parent, and also applies to ski rentals. In addition to researching on the Internet, it may be worth it to visit a library to browse through old issues of Ski Magazine.

Call your travel agent. Ski areas pay significant attention to their skier numbers. If bookings are low for certain time period, they will launch promotional campaigns with incredible package deals. Let your travel agent know you're interested and ask the agent to notify you if one becomes available. Also visit www.ski.com to find out about complete package rates and last minute bargains on a variety of resorts.

SKI WEAR

As far as what you wear, remember that you don't have to be a fashion model. There are thousands of people on the hill, and no one from the area will probably ever see you again. If they do, they won't recognize you without the ski goggles and hat. So if your jacket is a little—gasp—dated, it's okay, really. But if your pants don't fit, then invest in a new pair of black, waterproof pants. They'll match any future jacket you choose to buy.

If you don't ski every year, consider renting pants and a jacket. Rentals are available at a most ski shops. And don't forget to consider the mass merchant. Wal-Marts, when located in ski towns, have wised up to the needs of tourists and often sell ski pants, jackets, turtlenecks, gloves, mittens, hats, headbands, and even long johns. The selection tends to be better at the beginning of the year. Wal-Mart is also the place to buy the hand warmers and inexpensive memorabilia from the town.

Finally, if you have the opportunity, make friends with people who live in ski towns. They can save you a fortune.

CHEAP WAYS TO PREPARE TO TRAVEL

By Jason Boyett

Despite increased security measures and inevitable airport delays, travel is easier these days than it ever has been before. Even my grandmother—who still refers to her sofa as a "divan" and her freezer as an "icebox"—has purchased plane tickets and booked hotel reservations online. Thanks to the Internet, everything from Parisian hotel prices to Paraguayan bus schedules is no further away than our fingertips.

Unfortunately, planning a trip seems so easy now that we often don't give it the attention we should. At the click of a mouse, we can take care of all the major stuff—getting there, where to stay, what to do. Then we don't think about the trip again until it's time to leave. Lost in the easy shuffle of it all are the minor preparations that need to be made, the kinds of things that can keep a wonderful vacation from turning into a disaster. The Boy Scouts are right: being prepared makes things a lot easier.

Following, then, are a few cheap ways to prepare for traveling. Before you zip up your suitcase and head out the door, look over the tips below. They'll do much more than make sure you're ready to go—they'll help you save time, money, and most importantly, your sanity.

FINANCES

• Empty out your wallet and purse before leaving. Take only two credit cards, your ATM card, your driver's license and any other necessary information (insurance card, prescription card, etc.). Leave all other credit cards at home—including debit cards, which are not always accepted at some locations, and can be of limited use.

• Talk to your credit card company. By letting them know you'll be going on a trip, you can steer around potential bumps in the road, particularly if you're traveling to another country. They will be aware you'll be making charges there (which can speed up approvals), and can inform you as to your card's acceptability. They can make sure your PIN number will work in the countries you're visiting, and can give you an alternate phone number to call in case you need to reach them (some 800 numbers may not work from foreign locations). You can also find out if your company charges a currency conversion fee, which will help you decide which card is the most economical for making purchases.

• Plan to change money through banks. You'll do much better there as opposed to more convenient places like airport terminals or train or bus stations. In fact, it's a good idea to get a small amount of local currency before you leave home. Many banks offer exchange services that can provide you with foreign bills.

If you aren't converting all of your American dollars to local currency before you leave, make sure you bring along the new 100 and twenty dollar bills. Many foreign banks no longer take the old ones.

• If you're using travelers' checks, learn what procedures to follow should they become lost. Make a copy of each check before you go, and record the following information: serial numbers, denominations, date and location of purchase, and the phone number to call to report them missing. Keep this list with you, and cross out each check as you use it.

• Contact the issuer of your ATM card. Find out your daily limits and plan accordingly (you might need to ask to have your limit increased). Make sure your PIN number will work in foreign countries. And, on your trip, don't wait until money's tight to look for an ATM—there's no guarantee it will work when you find one.

• Use an extra check register for keeping up with your travel purchases, whether you're charging or paying with cash. Before you leave, decide upon a spending limit and keep track down to a zero balance.

• Bring lots of single dollar bills for tipping during airport transfers, courtesy shuttles, and hotels.

DOCUMENTATION

• Make photocopies of your trip's itinerary, including destination and dates. Put a copy of it into an outside pocket of each piece of luggage you're taking. If luggage gets lost or picked up by some guy with his nose in a guidebook, this will increase the chances of your being reunited with your stuff before the trip's over.

• Use a durable, protected ID card on your luggage rather than the paper and elastic ones provided by the airlines. More than 90 percent of lost luggage never makes it home because the staff of the airline, cruise ship, train, etc. can't figure out who owns it.

• Check the expiration date of your passport. Many countries won't let you enter if your passport is few months within expiration.

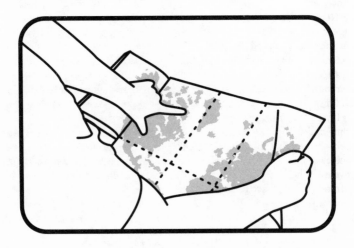

• Before you go, photocopy your passport, credit cards, driver's license, insurance policy numbers, vaccination certificates, airline tickets—everything you can think of. Keep at least one copy of each of these with you at all times. Give another copy to a friend at home who has access to a fax machine, in case you run into trouble. You might also want to scan each document and e-mail the digital files as attachments to your email account. Make sure you're with a provider that lets you access your inbox from anywhere in the world.

• Prepare a copy of your personal medical history. This should include: the name and address of your insurance company; emergency contacts; your blood type; your eyeglass prescription; a list of current medications (especially their generic names, since drug brands can vary internationally); a list of your allergies; a list of immunizations; and a basic description of your past and present medical condition.

PACKING

• Don't pack too much. Before you pack, lay out all the clothes you think you'll need. Then pack half of it. Make sure your clothing is comfortable and easy to clean. As a general rule, leather pants are not a good idea—even if you're not traveling.

• Pack everything in plastic bags. This is a lifesaver if you have to repack after having your luggage searched—or if your shampoo springs a leak during a flight.

• Never put prescription drugs or valuables in luggage to be checked. Keep these in your carry-on. To avoid customs delays, carry medication in its original packaging.

• Since everyone's luggage tends to look the same, tie a strip of cloth, ribbon, or yarn to your checked bags. You'll be able to spot them easier as they make their way around the carousel, and the aforementioned guy reading the Fodor's will think twice before grabbing it.

• If your luggage arrives damaged, or not at all, file a written report with the airline before leaving the airport. Let them know where you'll be for the next week—if your bags went to the wrong destination, it could take a few days. Once, on a trip to Brazil, my suitcase took an accidental side trip to Rome. When it eventually arrived in Sao Paulo three days later, the airline knew where to find me. I spent the rest of the week glaring jealously at my well-traveled soft side.

MISCELLANEOUS

- Buy film before you go. Tourist hotspots and amusement parks will sell it at a much higher price. The same applies for soft drinks, but those can be hard to pack.
- Cancel your newspaper, pay your bills, and arrange for someone to check your house or apartment occasionally (and get your mail) while you're away.
- Give all travel information to your family or close friends before you go. If anything should happen, they'll have a better chance of reaching you.
- Never travel in a new pair of shoes. You'll regret it. Either bring along comfortable stand-bys or break them in ahead of time.

Anyone who's been on a vacation knows they often can be as stressful as they are relaxing, particularly if something goes wrong. Unforeseen problems like lost luggage, documents or money can be especially costly. By following these suggestions, you can save more than your finances—you may save your entire vacation.

CHEAP WAYS TO ENJOY YOUR TRIP

By Margaret Feinberg

TRAVEL WITH FRIENDS

Traveling with friends, family, and loved ones can drastically reduce your traveling expenses. Driving together to the airport can save on parking. Renting a small house instead of a hotel room can save on lodging and the final bill. If enough people go with you, everyone can enjoy group discounts. If you're looking to make new friends, consider finding a travel companion at *www.travelchums.com* which links individuals of similar backgrounds and interests. The website *www.whytravelalone.com* provides similar services and helps single travelers avoid paying extra fees and rates. Beyond the savings, you'll be able to make and share memories with others for a lifetime.

DON'T BE HOSTILE TO HOSTELS

Hostelling International, *www.hiayh.org*, offers reasonable to downright cheap lodging all across the world. While the majority of hostels offer bunk beds and group living conditions, some provide private rooms and even breakfast for additional fees. Before booking a regular hotel or lodging reservation, visit Hostelling International's website to find out if there are any hostels in the area and the services they provide. Many times you'll meet new people, make new friends, and find discounts for activities in the area readily available. While youth enjoy free membership, adults can join for a low annual fee.

GO AT A SLOWER PACE

For the get-me-there-now experience, nothing beats an airplane, but depending on the distance, time of year, and airfare wars (or lack thereof), you may want to consider an alternative means of transportation. Depending on the cost of gasoline and the distance you want to travel, consider driving. Stay at campgrounds and hostels rather than hotels. Check into taking the bus in order to enjoy the scenic route without having to drive all those miles. Ask about "Go Anywhere" fares. Price train tickets as well. When you add up parking, airline travel, and incidentals in the airport, you may find that a slower mode of transportation is best and even more enjoyable.

NEGOTIATE

Negotiate, negotiate, negotiate. If you're travel plans are flexible, call hotels in the area you want to visit and ask about what you can do to lower the rates they're offering. They may ask you to stay an extra night or alter your stay by a few nights for significant savings. When you check into a hotel, ask if the rate you've been given is the best one available, and if any personal memberships, whether to AARP or AAA, can lower the rate.

After you've booked a car rental, continue calling back to see if the rates have dropped. As a general rule, you may want to avoid mentioning that you've already booked so they don't quote the same rate back to you.

GO ONLINE

A few hours on the Internet can add up to big savings and lots of information when you're planning a trip. For research, type in the key words of the destination and search for the city's local chamber of commerce to find out about upcoming activities and events. Also visit *www.frommers.com* and *www.fodors.com*. The web also offers a variety of opportunities to save money. Websites such as *www.gaswars.com* and *www.freetrip.com* can tell you which gas stations in your own area and in the one you're visiting are currently charging the lowest gas prices, saving you ten to twenty cents per gallon. The website *www.freetrip.com* can also help you avoid toll roads, select scenic routes, and find economy lodging.

If you're traveling to Europe, visit *www.easyrentacar.com*, an Internet-only firm that rents cars at reasonable rates in a number of European cities.

VISIT FRIENDS

Don't miss the opportunity to visit friends in resort destinations. Do you have friends living in Hawaii, a national park, a ski town, or overseas? If they offer you a bed, couch, or even floor space, take advantage of their offer. Not only will you be able to save on lodging, but you'll also have a local who can show you around and help give you an authentic visit.

TRAVEL TOWARD OFF-SEASON

Resort rates vary greatly throughout the year, and almost every location offers off-season prices. Often the lower rates are tied to weather conditions or the school calendar. Find out the dates and rates of the off-season in the place you want to travel, and make reservations for either the first or last two weeks of the off-season. You'll be able to enjoy the same amenities for much less.

KNOW IF ALL-INCLUSIVE IS FOR YOU

Some resorts are all-inclusive, with the exception of motorized vehicles. When booking a reservation, clarify exactly what is included in the hotel's price. A number of companies organize affordable, inclusive travel packages. Five star and grand tourist resorts often offer lower prices when you book several months ahead of your departure date, while three star resorts will often offer last-minute, reduced prices. If traveling to a third world country, you'll probably want to stay away from any resorts below three stars, at least on your first visit.

If you tend to eat and drink a lot, then the all-inclusive package is probably for you. The advantage of the all-inclusive is that you don't have to leave the resort. Huge buffets offer dozens of options, but even with so many choices you might be surprised to discover that after day three or so, all the food and drinks taste the same. If you're a light eater (and drinker), you're better off booking a reservation at a non-all-inclusive resort and exploring the markets and restaurants in the area you're visiting.

TRADE HOMES

If you're living in a desirable location, more than likely there's someone, somewhere living in another desirable location who would be willing to trade homes or apartments with you. For an annual fee, Trading Homes, Inc. will help link you with individuals across the world who want to trade their homes. Visit *www.trading-homes.com*.

BE SPONTANEOUS

Last minute deals lurk for the spontaneous, flexible traveler. Most travel websites offer a last minute deal listing. Sites such as *www.lasvegas.com*, *www.weekendwebsavers.com*, *www.choicehotels.com*, and *www.rentalcarguide.com* are just a few to explore. After finding a bargain on the web, go directly to the airline or hotel's home page and see if they offer comparable or even lower prices. Hotels will often offer last minute deals directly to customers without advertising throughout the travel industry. Websites aren't always updated regularly, so call or book online immediately to ensure the price.

CHEAP WAYS TO PLAN A CREATIVE DATE

By Josh Hatcher

What is better than being young and in love? Being young and in love with a couple extra dollars in your pocket. The Beatles said, "Money can't buy me love," and we all know that romance doesn't need jingle to bloom. Try these cheap and creative date ideas with your sweetheart.

CAR-LESS DRIVE-IN

As drive-in theaters become less common, a piece of Americana slips into oblivion. Recreate the fun Mom and Dad encountered by hauling your TV and VCR out to the backyard on a starry night with a blanket and some bug spray. The neighbors might think it strange, but you'll have a blast.

SKIP DINNER

Eat dinner at home. Later, go out for Krispy Kreme or Dunkin' Donuts. Stop at the ice cream parlor. Just get a snack together, which is definitely cheaper than a whole meal.

Instead of going out late, get up before work or class and go out for breakfast. Or meet each other at your favorite restaurant for lunch. Most restaurants have lunch and breakfast specials, and it's cheaper than going out for dinner.

WATCH THE PAPER

Most communities have a free newspaper or website that lists fine arts events and festivals in the area. You might find a place to take free clogging lessons or to see a junior high ballet or choral concert. When local communities sponsor festivals, you can browse the vendors' tables, get cheap hot dogs from a youth group and maybe even see a live bluegrass band.

DRESS UP

Dress up nice, like it's a date to Carnegie Hall. Even if it's dinner at McD's, how grand would it be to eat cheeseburgers in fancy clothes?

GET WILD

The admission fee at your local zoological park is probably less than five bucks a head. You can spend the whole day watching the monkeys pick lice out of each other's heads, or you can just walk around and enjoy the landscaping.

The wild animals can lead for some pretty interesting conversation, and conversation can help you get to know each other better—which is why you are dating, right?

SHOWER IN THE MIDDLE OF THE NIGHT

Watch the news for the next big meteor shower. They usually peak at some odd hour of the night like 3 A.M. So meet each other at the park, or in the backyard and watch the shooting stars. Even if there is no meteor shower, just stargazing late at night would be very romantic.

COFFEESHOP-IT

Live music and poetry readings, with a three-dollar cover and a two-dollar cappuccino is quite romantic. You can sit there all night. Just drink slowly. It's a great atmosphere—calm and laid back, and perfect for conversation.

If they have an open mic night, write a silly love song or poem and surprise your date with a performance. Even if you have no talent, the sentiment of making a fool out of yourself to say, "I love you," is a very romantic experience.

EVERYDAY LIFE

When you have to run to Wal-Mart to pick up toothpaste or drop by the post office to mail off bills, make a date of it. Not that a trip to the dentist is a particularly romantic experience, but it's a great way to get to know your date. In a dating relationship, people often put their best foot forward, and it's easy to give someone a false impression. Doing everyday things together is a great way to see each other for who you really are, and it might even offer some of the most unexpected romantic moments.

LOOK AT OLD STUFF

Go to a museum. They are inexpensive or free. Spend some time walking through the exhibits, and talk about it. Talk quietly, though, or they will kick you out.

History has a very romantic appeal to it. While the dinosaur bones may not be that romantic, spend some time in the medieval section and talk about chivalry. Or look at the World War 2 section and find some pictures of love hungry sailors, and then take turns making love hungry faces at each other.

MY PLACE OR YOURS?

Cook each other dinner. Or cook dinner together. Have a blast by going to the grocery store together first. Pick out some exotic food neither of you has tried before. Restaurants are expensive, and for the cost of dining out once, you could probably make two or three dinners at home.

GROUP DATE

Get 17 billion friends and go to the park and play ultimate Frisbee, or go jump in a swimming hole together. The more people, the more fun you can have. Romance doesn't have to be limited to when you are alone. It's also great for first dates. If you don't like your date, there are tons of other people you can hang out with.

If you all go out to dinner together and ask for separate checks, you will definitely frazzle the waitress, which isn't good. So to make it easier on the restaurant industry, order pizza and a pitcher of Pepsi, and then have everybody pitch in an equal amount at the end of the night. For a large group of friends who pile into a diner, file into separate booths. Split up by couples or foursomes. It will be less overwhelming than trying to seat forty-three people at one table.

THE GREAT OUTDOORS

Picnics, hikes, sunset walks, swimming at the beach or a community pool, bike riding: Who says a date has to mean dinner and a movie? Spend some time connecting with the great outdoors and each other.

Watch a sunset, lay out a blanket in the park and snuggle and read. Go boating at the lake. Go dancing in the rain, or puddle hopping. Wake up early and watch the sunrise at the beach.

For thousands of years, restaurants and movie theaters were non-existent, and people still dated and romanced each other. Love poets from Solomon to Shakespeare compared their lovers to the beauty in nature. Their inspiration had to have come from somewhere!

CHEAP WAYS TO SAY I LOVE YOU

By Josh Hatcher

Cliché gifts and commercialized products take the personal touch out of saying "I love you" on special occasions. Plus, florists jack up the price of roses and chocolate for any holiday and seasonal excuse they can find. Sometimes the best way to show you care is in simple and small ways. Here are a few:

SNAIL MAIL

We send emails and IM each other incessantly. We carry on fourteen conversations with people in fourteen different states instantaneously. The buzz gets old. So take the time to write an encouraging note on a postcard, piece of paper, or napkin; spend the thirty-seven cents (or whatever the ever-growing rate is) and send it via the postal service. Even if you live in the same town or even the same house, something deep within us all longs to open the mailbox and see something other than credit card offers and bills.

SACRIFICE

Each of us has something we hate to do that our loved one likes. My wife likes baked things. I hate to bake. But every now and then, I'll pull out all the stops and bake a "goodie" for her. Think about what your loved one likes that you really don't enjoy, and then roll up your sleeves and do it, even if you can't write a poem, paint a picture, bake a cake, or hate playing cards. If you do it lovingly, I guarantee you'll get an "A" for effort!

DO IT YORSELF

Make your own card. Write your own song. Make a birdhouse yourself. Instead of spending the money, spend the time to do something special. Even the least creative person has something they can make as an offering to the one they love.

DINNER CHEAP

Don't spend thirty bucks just to eat fancy. Get takeout Chinese and eat it at a drive-in theater. Cook cheap steak and eat it on the patio with a makeshift canopy of white Christmas lights. Invite a zillion friends over for a surprise party, and tell them all to bring a bag of chips and a cheap dollar store gift for your loved one that says, "We all love you."

TECHNO-LOVE

Log on to one of those annoying animated greeting card sites. Download a bunch of pretty love songs and burn a romantic CD. Scan in your favorite pictures together and make a website declaring your love for each other to the world.

SECRET ADMIRER

Romance needs to stay alive even after you get married. Start writing letters, juicy, steamy mushy stuff you might find in a dime store romance novel, and make up a pen name. Your honey will of course suspect you, but just smile and keep it secret as long as you can. You will drive your lover mad, and someday soon when the truth is told, the prank will have a profoundly romantic effect.

SCAVENGER HUNT

Send your loved one on a scavenger hunt all over town to places of significance to you both. Place a clue at each location to get them to the next place. The last clue can send them to your favorite coffee shop or pizza place where you sit anxiously waiting.

HIDE AND SEEK

Hide cards and presents in out of the way locations, like the freezer, or in a box of cereal. Hide it in a suit pocket, or in a pair of swanky dress shoes. If your date is not a smoker, hide a love note in the ashtray if his or her car. Eventually your little message will be found, and love will abound.

IN A TREE

Go for a walk in the woods. Climb a tree together. Or lay out a blanket in the shade under a tree and read together. Before you leave, carve your initials in the tree trunk with a jackknife.

SCRAPBOOK

Collect all the letters and cards and notes you have sent each other, all your pictures together, the ticket stubs from memorable movies or concerts that you attended together, or any other significant doodads, and assemble a scrapbook. Leave it on your coffee table and show it to friends.

TWO STRAWS

Go to the local diner, and order an extra large milkshake, with two straws. It's cheaper than two milkshakes, and it's a classic romance move. You might even get a smooch in between sips.

KISSES

Buy a bag of Hershey's Kisses, take out all the flags, and replace them with messages you have written yourself. If you want your sweetie to notice them on their own, try using bright paper to get their attention.

ONE HUNDRED QUESTIONS

Getting to know each other is a very important part of being in love. So getting to know each other better is a great way to express love. Start making a list of questions you have always wanted to ask each other. If you have been dating a while, write down the answers that you think your sweetheart will give.

When your list grows to fifty questions for each of you, take an evening, go out to dinner, and ask your list of questions to each other, share the answers that you guessed with each other, and remember the answers they do give. It's a great way to learn about the person you love.

SAY IT

This is a hard one for a lot of men in particular. Just say, "I love you," every day. It won't kill you. Actions do speak louder than words, but the words reinforce and stimulate love. It also helps to remind yourself sometimes that you do love this person. Love is not an emotion; it is an action. When you are so angry that you could throw a brick, say it out loud. Remind yourself that you have chosen to love this person, even if you don't feel like it. Of course, if you say it, be prepared to follow through. Love means sacrifice, putting each other first, and letting go of our own pride. So if saying that you love this person means that you are willing to follow through even when you don't feel mushy inside, then you have just truly demonstrated it.

SPEND TIME

Time is precious. It is valuable. And when we invest time in relationships, it usually returns with deeper friendships, stronger love, and wonderful memories. Just sit together, telling stories, listening to each other, growing your friendship. You cannot love someone if you have not first been friends. So take the time to grow that friendship. If it grows well, it will last even if the romance does not.

CHEAP WAYS TO PROPOSE

By Jason Boyett

First, a disclaimer: The purpose of the following paragraphs is not—not—to convince any would-be question-poppers to skimp on the actual hardware. Guys, do not buy a cut-rate ring. Your future wife will have it forever, and when you're forty, you don't want to be thinking, "Man, was I a cheapo." Follow the two months' salary rule, or whatever guidelines you and your significant other choose. But get a good ring. This is not "Cheap Ways to Score an Engagement Ring."

Having said that, ladies, feel free to move on to the next chapter, unless you're Monica to her Chandler and are considering taking matters into your own hands. The rest is pretty much for the guys. Let's continue.

A brief perusal of how-to-be-romantic books and women's magazines will tell you that no small number of married women carry a certain secret with them, the admission that their marriage proposal was less romantic than they'd hoped. This is a serious suggestion, considering the fact that most of the women I know have been fantasizing about this event since they were old enough to drape a bed sheet over their heads and pretend it was a veil. Yet when the occasion finally arrives, a surprising amount of women are actually disappointed—not in the result, of course, but in the presentation.

FIRST, A DISCLAIMER:

PLACE RING HERE

That's not all. I've spoken to a variety of married women—and by "variety" I mean my wife and my sister-in-law and a couple of their friends—and this is what they tell me: just spending a lot of money on the proposal doesn't necessarily mean you're doing it right. Ouch. You could blow $300 on a limousine and a five-course meal and still not give her the meaningful and romantic moment she's been waiting for.

Why? Because any guy can make reservations at *Le Floofy-Floo*. And any bonehead with a credit card can rent a limo. All either requires is a little cash. What makes a proposal memorable to your bride-to-be is its uniqueness, the idea that no one could have pulled this off but you. It's the knowledge that, at the chosen moment, she is the only person in the world having this very experience. That means something—and it has nothing to do with money.

First things first. A good marriage proposal is equal parts creativity, personality, and thoughtfulness. The creativity will catch your partner off-guard, rising above her already high expectations. It will thrill her. A proposal with personality assures your future bride that you didn't just find this idea in, say, some book about doing things cheaply (um … feel free to tear these pages out after you've read them). The thoughtfulness makes her feel special—she'll know you've spent weeks and weeks doing everything you can to make the moment memorable.

That said, here are some suggestions. Make them your own. Mix and match. Blend them up with your personality and that of your partner, and see what you end up with. Just keep in mind the attributes listed above.

MESSAGE IN A BOTTLE (Long-form idea)

I heard the story once of a guy (we'll call him Pete) who met his steady girlfriend on a beach in North Carolina. They fell in love, and eventually began talking about marriage. When he decided it was time to set things in motion, he prepared for it a month in advance by purchasing a Swiss Army Knife—the kind with a small corkscrew. He talked about how every guy should carry a pocketknife, and made sure his girlfriend was aware of it (which would have prevented her from becoming suspicious had she accidentally discovered it later in the story). The month passed quickly, and on the day of their one-year anniversary, Pete casually suggested driving over to the beach where they first met. She agreed, and they packed up a simple picnic dinner and headed out. After the picnic, Pete and his girlfriend decided to take a walk along the shoreline. As they reached the place where they'd met twelve months earlier, he noticed a simple bottle that appeared to have just washed up in the surf. (Of course, Pete had meticulously planned everything beforehand, and had arranged for an accomplice to secretly tail them to the beach. The accomplice raced ahead of them during the walk, planting the bottle to make sure it was bobbing in the water, but not too far out from shore). She picked it up, noticing a piece of paper in it. The bottle was sealed with a cork. Aha! Pete pulled out his trusty corkscrew. She opened the bottle, unfolded the paper, and read: "Close your eyes and count to three. Pete has something for you." When she opened her eyes, of course, Pete was down on one knee, ring extended.

She said yes.

All it cost Pete was some time and planning, plus the pocketknife and the old bottle. Creativity (the bottle), personality (the note) and thoughtfulness (the location, the date, the prior planning)—all the requirements were there. That's how you do it.

Now, short-form ideas:

THE ROMANTIC MOVIE

Secretly procure a VHS tape of her favorite romantic movie. Copy it onto a videotape of your own. Midway through the copy, stop the movie, and record yourself speaking to her on camera. *Don't pop the question on the tape.* Instead, say something transitional about your love, about the relationship, about your future (the prelude stuff). Then, on the day itself, make a pretense of renting a movie. Make popcorn, curl up on the couch, and slide in the video. She'll be astonished when Meg Ryan disappears only to be replaced by your face on the screen. When she comes to her senses, she'll notice you've dropped to one knee. The ring will slide right on, because her fingers will be buttery from the popcorn.

THE TREASURE HUNT

If your partner likes a little do-it-yourself fun, send her on a wild goose chase. You'll be playing the role of the goose. Have a simple bouquet of flowers delivered to her, with a note attached. On that note, give her a clue that will send her to a destination that's meaningful to both of you. Then repeat the process. At each destination, arrange for her to receive a small gift and another clue (the gifts need not be expensive ones, just thoughtful—a piece of her favorite candy, a single flower, a love note). Keep the process short—four or five destinations will be enough. The final clue will lead her to a romantic dinner you'll have prepared yourself, where the rest is up to you.

THE RIBBON

Find a long, red ribbon. It doesn't have to be velvet, but it needs to be substantial enough to seem luxurious. Tie one end to her doorway, so that she sees it upon arriving home. Every five or ten feet, attach a note telling her one thing you love about her—make these serious, funny, sexy, or some combination of the three. At the end of the ribbon (and out of sight from the doorway), set up a room full of votive candles. Shut the door. Dim the lights. Drop to a knee and wait.

THE EASTER EGG HUNT

Write out the phrase "Will you marry me?" on four Easter eggs, then scatter them in her yard or a favorite park. Make sure the "marry" egg is the hardest to find. You might want to throw in a few additional verbs, just for fun—something like *poke, drop-kick, hug*. On Easter morning, deliver an egg-gathering basket with a note attached, telling her where to start. Once she finds all the eggs and arranges them into the proper sequence, show up with a final egg—one of those plastic ones for putting candy inside. That's where the ring goes.

THE TAN

This is a truly original approach. Purchase some sunscreen—the kind that comes in an applicator stick works best—and write "Marry Me" on your stomach or back. If you need it, get a friend to help. Then take her to the lake or beach. Spend the day with your shirt off, trying to get a minor sunburn or a decent tan. At the end of the day, your darkened skin will have stenciled in the words. Show it to the appropriate party, and have the ring ready.

There are as many ways to get engaged as there are to meet your partner. All it takes is a little imagination and careful planning. The best thing is, proposing marriage doesn't have to cost a fortune. In fact, the best proposals probably don't.

CHEAP WAYS TO PLAN A WEDDING

By Josh Hatcher and Margaret Feinberg

The most important day of your life together lurks around the corner, ready to suck you or your parents like a cash vampire, leaving a trail of receipts and birdseed clear to the altar. Why spend tens of thousands, when all that matters is the "I do"? The thing is, our culture places so much emphasis on the fairy-tale wedding that people forget about the important part: the marriage itself. So with that in mind, here are some ways to save for that house down payment or to get married without relying on a healthy dowry, while keeping the emphasis on a healthy marriage at the forefront of the whole event.

ASK AND YOU WILL RECEIVE

You already have a hundred or more friends and family members who are asking you what you want for your wedding present. Ask them to donate flowers, or to make their famous avocado-filled cucumber cups or a wedding cake. Chances are someone has a friend who takes decent pictures. After all, they're going to spend twenty-five bucks on another blender unless you give them some direction.

USED DRESSES

I know, girls, you always dreamed of that fairy tale Vera Wang, but after all, the other dresses were only worn once right? If you go to a consignment shop, you might find a display model that has never been worn at a tenth of the cost. Get your grandmother to alter it for you, and voila—custom fit, dream dress. Now you only need something new, something borrowed, and something blue.

INVITATIONS

Stop at Staples and buy some pretty parchment paper, then use a greeting card program to design and print your own invitations from your computer. You can write a poem, use a calligraphy font, scan in a personal photo, and make unique invitations that will have people talking for weeks. Print off a master copy on plain white paper, and have Staples copy them for you. It's cheaper than ink for your printer. You can also cut costs by using postcards for RSVPs. Skip those annoying envelopes, and the postage is cheaper.

TUXES

Definitely rent, don't buy. When you do go to pick your tuxedo out, keep in mind that no one is going to be looking at the elaborate-ness of the groom's tuxedo. The focus is going to be on the bride. So get the most basic and cheapest one you can find, and even then shop around, because it is bound to be cheaper at one store than it is at another. Check with you tuxedo renter to see if there are any discounts. For example: rent three, get one free. Also check to see if there are any fees if it is not returned by a certain time, or a fee to get your measurements. (If there is, find out what measurements they need, and have somebody else measure you for free).

GET MARRIED ON A WEEKDAY

If you really want to skimp, reception halls are always cheaper on weekdays, your preacher might give you a discount, and you're sure to have fewer people show up, so your catering bill will be less.

KEEP IT SIMPLE

The church probably has its own architectural beauty. Don't overdo it. A couple flowers, a couple bows and ribbons, and a few colored napkins should be enough. If you decorate too much, they'll never even notice the groom's new haircut or the flower girl's pretty bow.

FLOWERS

Don't order rare Tahitian orchids. Order daisies or carnations. Keep it as simple as possible. Instead of the bridesmaids each carrying a whole bouquet, have them each carry a single rose. Limit the flowers to a few centerpieces, and simple bouquets where absolutely needed. You may even buy the flowers and have the bridesmaids help arrange them the night before. Bulk flowers are definitely cheaper than flower arrangements. If you don't know how to arrange flowers, visit the library and borrow a book with some pointers and tips.

KEEP IT SHORT

Don't go for an all-night reception. Instead of having a wild party and dancing 'til the wee hours of the morning, reserve the reception hall for a few hours, have a simple reception, and send the guests on their way. You might even have the reception in the church fellowship hall. You already are reserving it for the wedding, it'll probably be a few dollars more, and if you keep it simple, you'll save a bundle.

HOTELS

To save your out-of-town guests a bit on hotel room costs, call ahead and make arrangements with a local hotel; they may give you a discount for bringing in business. Just be sure to let your guests know the hotel information in the invitation.

ELOPE

It's not for everyone, but if the two of you are overwhelmed by all the details and you just want to get married, why spend all the money? If you really want your family and friends to be there, tell them when and where it will be, and let them know that they can support you by showing up. It doesn't matter if the wedding vows are set in a massive cathedral or a backyard or in the office of a Justice of the Peace; what matters is whether the marriage vows are spoken and kept for the rest of your lives.

PREMARITAL COUNSELING

Although it may be an extra expense, premarital counseling with a minister or professional marriage counselor is a must. Take the time to learn about the marriage commitment before getting swept up in all the details of flower arranging and tuxedo fittings. After all, a wedding is one day. A marriage is supposed to last forever. Take the extra time to cultivate your commitment. Advice from an experienced married couple or trained counselor can save your marriage later. A healthy, satisfying marriage is worth every penny spent on counseling if it gives you the tools to keep your marriage together.

FAVORS, PLEASE

If there was ever a time to call in all those favors you've been storing up, your wedding is the event. Look for friends and family who can use their talent or service as a gift to you. Do you have a friend who can take pictures? Do you know someone who loves to bake and is willing to take on the challenge of creating a masterpiece cake? Do you have friends in a band? A family member who loves to make home movies?

Friends and family members can offer a variety of services. From actually conducting the ceremony to singing, you probably know someone who can offer their service as a wedding gift. After the event, send a thank you card and small appreciation gift. You may also want to consider bartering for services. What services can you offer? They key is to find a trade that both parties can appreciate.

CUTTING DOWN ON CATERING

The catering bill is one of the largest expenses when organizing a wedding. A large portion of that bill will be determined by how many people are invited to the reception and what time of day you choose to hold it. If you're married in the morning, you can plan on a moderately priced brunch or lunch, while an early afternoon ceremony can be followed by an economical cake and punch reception with light appetizers. Late afternoon weddings are usually followed by a dinner, which is one of the pricier catering options. Another option is an evening wedding followed by a desert reception, though additional hors d'oeuvres are appreciated by most guests. Holiday weddings tend to be more expensive, because the staff has to be paid overtime.

It's important to shop around for a good but affordable caterer. Talk to friends who have either recently been married or attended a wedding for recommendations. Blindly flipping open the Yellow Pages can be dangerous, but if you stumble upon a reasonably-priced caterer with a good reputation, it's time to set up an appointment.

In addition to asking for references, ask if you can attend one of the weddings they cater. It will provide an opportunity to preview their presentation of food, which is often just as important, if not more important, than the food itself. Smaller catering companies tend to be more flexible in working with individuals and can prove to be more sensitive to your pocket book. Let them know your budget limitations at the beginning of your meeting and ask what they can provide. Negotiate smaller items and find out what they will let you provide. Can friends and family members bring additional dishes, prepare appetizers such as vegetable plates, or mix iced tea and lemonade in five-gallon dispensers? Those little things can really add up.

As a general rule, though, you don't want to scrimp on the actual food. Nothing is worse than running out of food or paying for unappetizing fare. You're better off shaving down the guest list and shopping around again for another caterer. Consider holding your wedding at a hotel with an all-inclusive rate. Many of these have special rates and programs for the wedding party.

Ask to see a copy of the total projected costs before agreeing to any contracts. Look for excessive rental fees from caterers who own their own dishes. Ask to see the dishes and flatware to ensure the expense is worthwhile. How many staff people are included in the price? Generally, one staff person is recommended for every fifty people, with more servers needed for sit down meals. Make sure gratuity and sales tax are included, since this can be a large add-on. Smaller fees such as corking fees and cake cutting fees can be negotiated. Also ask about additional costs if the reception runs over time. Don't forget to find out about final payments, cancellation policies, refunds, and when the final guest count is due.

Also ask who gets to keep the extra food. This can be a blessing to the bride's family as well as the couple as they head out on their honeymoon.

If the catering bill is still out of reach, consider organizing a picnic, barbecue or potluck. A taco bar or pasta station can be a fun, casual way to feed guests. A buffet of ranch rolls, luncheon meats, cheeses, and a few side dishes works well, too. Shop at Sam's Club or Costco and buy food in bulk.

HAVING A CAKE AND EATING IT TOO

If you don't have someone who can bake a cake for you, it's worth comparison-shopping for this precious dessert. Prices vary widely from shop to shop. Ask to see photos, and inquire about the quality of ingredients. Consider ordering a cake through your regular bakery. They may offer you a discount.

Remember that simpler designs are less expensive. A stacked three-layer cake with butter cream frosting is easier and quicker to prepare, which is reflected in the final bill. You can save expenses by ordering a basic cake and adding additional decorations—such as greenery, flowers, pearl necklaces, ribbon, or chocolate—yourself. You may also want to consider ordering a smaller decorated cake for presentation and have friends prepare several plain sheet cakes. Have the decorated cake cut in the back, and guests won't know whether their piece came from the display cake or the homemade ones.

As an alternative, you may work with friends to create a cookie table. Simply have four or five friends commit to baking two dozen cookies for each other's weddings. When it's your wedding, you won't have to bake and can enjoy all their goodies displayed on a cookie table. With the extra confections, you can order a smaller wedding cake.

Try to pick up the cake yourself or have someone else pick it up in order to save delivery charges. And have a sweet time!

CHEAP WAYS TO PLAN A HONEYMOON

By Josh Hatcher

Ah, the joys of marital bliss. There's nothing like taking a week or two off work to enjoy the company of your new spouse. Somewhere along the line, though, someone got the great idea that a honeymoon had to include a cruise ship, a trip to an exotic island and a terrible rash of spending. What is the sense in racking up hundreds or thousands of dollars in debt as your wedding gift to each other? The honeymoon should be a stress-free vacation in which all the joys of your nuptials are given sanctuary from the rest of the world. This is for those out there who want to spend the honeymoon enjoying their spouse instead of a new line of credit.

TWO NIGHTS IN A HOTEL

When people ask what you need for a wedding gift, ask them for a night at a hotel. You don't have to have a honeymoon suite; you don't need a heart-shaped jacuzzi. But you definitely want at least two nights in a hotel.

REGISTER

People register at department stores and shopping malls for wedding gifts. If you want to make your honeymoon special, you can register at *www.honeyluna.com*, where your loved ones can contribute to your honeymoon directly. Even if you just let people know that helping you out with your honeymoon is what you want for your wedding gift, it can make a dent in your travel costs.

CAMP

My wife and I canoed out to a deserted island in the Chesapeake Bay and camped out for three nights. I was very grateful that we had spent our first few nights together in a comfortable bed, but the camping trip was spectacular. There was no one around; it was secluded, romantic, and memorable. Roughing it may not be your idea of a great time. If you have to have a shower every day, and can't build a fire, or pitch a tent, you probably want to pick some other way to celebrate the freshness of your matrimony.

PACK A BASKET

You might not feel like leaving for dinner. Chances are, you won't get much to eat at the reception, will get hungry, and won't feel like putting clothes on to go out to dinner. Honestly, you may be so worn out from your wedding and the reception that all you want to do is sleep. So pack a basket with some candy, and crackers and cheese, and candles, maybe a bottle of sparkling grape juice and a couple of dollar store glasses. Think about what food you can take along that gives you energy, doesn't have to be refrigerated, and that both of you enjoy. You might even hide some sexy underwear in the bottom. Stash it in your getaway car as a present for your spouse.

STAY HOME

A few days in your new home together, with the ringer turned off, and the shades pulled, can be a very romantic and exciting adventure, and it won't cost you much at all. Rent movies, order take-out, and cut off all modes of communication for a few days. Even if you come home from your tropical paradise a few days early and spent the rest of the week at home, imagine the money you'll save!

GENERIC RETREATS

If you really want to get away, and experience a spectacular honeymoon, you can still do it, as long as you settle for the generic version. Go to a lesser-traveled resort town, or find a bed and breakfast in the middle of nowhere.

If you've always wanted to go to Europe, and you cannot afford even a semblance of the cost, then check out Busch Gardens in Williamsburg, Virginia. If an island vacation is your cup of tea, then try the Outer Banks of North Carolina, or the Florida Keys instead of Jamaica or St. Thomas.

Really, any off-season destination would be tremendously romantic simply because it is your honeymoon. Try a ski resort in the summer, or a waterfront cottage in the winter. The price will be at rock bottom, and it helps you pay more attention to your spouse without the expensive attractions and distractions.

PLANES, TRAINS, AND AUTOMOBILES

Not only should you carefully choose your destination, but your mode of getting there. If you have your honeymoon nearby, then driving there together would be easier and more efficient. If you must travel long distances, weigh the options of air travel over bus and rail. You may be able to afford a more exciting location if you take a little longer to get there.

SCHEDULE EARLY

If you can make all your calls several months in advance, you can often lock in lower rates on hotels, cruise packages, and airfare. You may even consider a travel agent that can get you set up with some great rates (they do high volume, and often get a discount because of it). It also takes a ton of stress off of your already overloaded wedding planning tray, and saving aggravation is a great way to cut costs. Aggravation leads to burn out, and if you can save money on inevitable therapists and psychiatrists, then by all means, get your planning done early, and if you want, have someone else do it.

The truth is, the honeymoon is all about enjoying your new spouse, and getting to know your mate more intimately than before. The places, the events, the dinning out, the resorts, and all that jazz are secondary to the romance, the passion, and the memories made with your loved one.

CHEAP WAYS TO HAVE A BABY

By Josh Hatcher

Actually, there is no cheap way to have a baby. It takes sweat and toil and cash beyond comprehension. But if you wait until you can afford to have kids, you'll never have them. Here are a few ways to ease the finances so that you can enjoy your new baby.

GET HELP

Get health insurance. Doctor bills are ridiculously expensive. If you cannot afford health insurance, most states have a health assistance program for lower and middle-income families. We all pay taxes, and one of the reasons that we do so is to help people who need to be helped. So don't feel guilty about asking for assistance if your family needs it.

WIC

WIC, or Women, Infants, and Children, is an often-misunderstood program. Most people equate it with public assistance, and really have no clue how it is structured. The program is designed to help middle and low-income families with educational resources and food. Each month they weigh and measure your child, to make sure that they are growing healthy, and to provide statistical data. They also offer checks each month that are redeemable at local grocery stores for milk, eggs, cheese, cereal, and peanut butter. The food that is given away is based on surplus. It's basically the food that gets thrown out because typically, a certain amount of milk and eggs and cheese is not sold by the "sell by" date on the package. That food would normally be thrown out. So, the government basically gives that surplus to help women, infants and children. Pregnant and nursing mothers, and any children under five years of age are eligible for the program if their income is not too high, although the income limits are surprisingly high, making the program available for many families who make a moderate income.

GET IT USED

The baby industry is making a killing. Apparently there are people in the world who want only the best for their child. The rest of us go to yard sales and thrift or second-hand stores, and our kids have everything they need, while keeping the credit card balance low. Besides, is anybody really going to notice that your baby is wearing Tommy Hilfiger? Babies look cute in anything. Don't waste your money. If you really want your kid to wear the best clothes, look for yard sales in the rich section of town.

BREASTFEED IF POSSIBLE

Doctors agree that it is healthier for the baby, and your checkbook will concur after the money saved on formula. Not everyone can do it. If you don't think you can, or are having problems, contact your pediatrician, and see if they have any information, or if they can get you in contact with a breastfeeding support group that can help you. If you determine that you cannot breastfeed, don't feel guilty, but try to apply for WIC, as they do provide formula in their program if you qualify. You can also save money by buying formula in bulk, clipping coupons, and accepting free samples wherever they are offered.

DIAPERS

Some diapers are better than others, but most are virtually identical. Store brands are often several dollars cheaper, with little or no lack of quality. It is usually cheaper to buy in bulk, but it's a good idea to bring a calculator and figure the cost per diaper. If the smaller pack is on sale, it may be worth it to buy six of the small packs rather than one super mega pack. Once your baby starts sleeping through the night, waking him up to change a wet diaper is like signing a no-sleep warrant. Buy one pack of premium super absorbent diapers to help your baby through the night, and during the day, the cheap variety will do just fine.

WIPES

We found a great way to save money on baby wipes: Make your own. It doesn't take that much work, and the wipes only cost about a tenth of the amount of store-bought wipes. They are strong and work just as well. Here's the recipe:

- Cut one roll of premium paper towels (the strongest ones you can find on sale) in half, and remove cardboard tube.

- Put each half in its own gallon size freezer bag.

- In a pitcher, mix two cups of warm water with one tablespoon of baby oil and two tablespoons of baby shampoo or baby bath.

- You can add aloe or other lotions as needed, then pour evenly over paper towels, letting liquid soak into towels. Pull wipes from the center of roll for each use.

BABY FOOD

If you don't have one, invest in a blender. Baby food sold in jars is a wonderful thing to have, as it does make life more convenient. However, instead of fifty cents for a jar of green beans, spend one dollar on a bag of frozen green beans. There are a lot of ways to store it, but one method is to cook the vegetables, blend them up, and then pour the frappe into ice cube trays. When the freeze, remove them and place them in a freezer bag. Depending on your child's appetite, you may need to pop two or three cubes in the microwave for each meal. You can do the same method with any vegetable, and also meats and stews, and anything else that your baby eats. Try to give the baby the same basic foods the rest of the family eats for dinner, minus the spices and the foods that the little one cannot digest yet.

LIFESTYLE CHANGES

With kids in the house, change is inevitable. Re-prioritize, and adjust your daily activities and expenses with the intent of doing what is best for your family. Trade in the Mustang for a mini-van. Swap the stellar career commitment for the slightly lower-paying job that lets you spend more time at home. Consider whether the cost of childcare is actually worth sending both parents back to work. A baby takes a lot of time, a lot of love, and a lot of sacrifice, but it is a beautiful trade. For each comfort and indulgence traded, a parent-child moment is made that will brighten the rest of your life.

CHEAP WAYS TO HELP THE NEEDY

By Jason Boyett

"Give a man a fish and he'll eat for a day. Teach a man to fish and he'll eat for a lifetime." No doubt you've heard the axiom before. It's often used to condemn no-strings-attached giving to the poor. Cliché or not, it paints a nice picture. Unfortunately, it only paints half the picture—it's great to teach a man to fish, but if the man has no fishing gear and no water nearby, *how* do you expect the knowledge of how to fish to do anything for him?

That's the plight of the poor. As it is for millions of people across the planet, poverty is a problem in the United States as well. The 2000 U.S. Census indicated that more than 30 million Americans live below the poverty line. Nearly half of those are children. And while dealing with the problem of poverty involves "helping the poor to help themselves," we need to remember that such a solution is long-term. What are we to do in the short-term? It's far too easy to get caught up in the politics and methodology of helping the poor while forgetting that you can contribute something yourself. In fact, a number of recent surveys have indicated that today's younger generation gives less to charity than any previous generation. Is it because we don't care? Or is it because we think someone else ought to be doing it—someone like Bill Gates, who could feed and shelter every homeless person in America for a month without making a dent in his wallet?

Did you pay for this book? If so, it's doubtful you fall below the poverty line. Most likely, you have something to give. You can't alleviate the problem by yourself; no one can. But what you can do is distribute some grace to your corner of the world. The thing to remember is that helping the poor isn't just about donating money. It's about meeting needs. Here's what you can do:

HOMELESS SHELTERS

If you live in a city of any size, there is probably at least one homeless shelter that helps people with meals, beds, hygiene, and other services. Most shelters welcome volunteers for a number of activities, from preparing and distributing meals to working in the business office.

FOOD BANKS

Surveys indicate up to 40 percent of people serviced by community food banks at one time or another, had to decide between eating and paying rent. If that's a decision you've never had to make, why not find a way to help out? Community food banks are instrumental in assisting the poor in your community, particularly around the holidays. They employ volunteers to sort and collect salvaged food (much of which comes from area supermarkets), distribute bread, manage inventory, and perform office tasks. You can help by doing the above or by organizing and giving to inventory builders like canned food drives.

SWEATERS

A few years ago, the inspirational magazine *Guideposts* came up with a unique way to help the poor knitting sweaters for them. Over the last four years, more than 120,000 children's sweaters have been knitted by volunteers in the U.S., Canada, Australia, and even New Guinea. If you can knit or crochet, *Guideposts* will be happy to give you a pattern. Don't know how to knit? They'll even hook you up with instructions. For more on the project, check out *www.guideposts.org*.

HABITAT FOR HUMANITY

Since 1976, Habitat has built in excess of one hundred thousand simple houses across the world for families lacking adequate shelter. A non-denominational, non-profit organization, Habitat sells its houses via interest-free mortgages. The homes are built by the homeowners themselves and a team of volunteers. If you have any sort of construction, electrical, or plumbing skills, you're exactly the kind of volunteer help Habitat needs. For those who don't know a Philips from a flathead, Habitat projects provide a fun, unintimidating environment to learn—all the while helping a very appreciative family. Contact your local chapter, or visit *www.habitat.org*.

CLOTHING & NECESSITIES

Most of us have far too many clothes—in our closet, stuff we haven't worn in years. When you run out of space, resist the urge to sell your old clothing on consignment or in garage sales. Instead, donate it to a charity like the Salvation Army or its equivalent. My wife and I worked one weekend a few years ago with a downtown women's center, the kind of place where battered women stay until they get their lives back together. We discovered the center was always in need of decent women's clothing, in addition to baby supplies and kids' clothes. After that weekend, Aimee cleaned out her closet immediately. If you have a full closet or baby clothes you'll never use again, why not give them to someone who'll treasure them?

BE THOUGHTFUL

It's easy in today's society to ignore the wizened drifters holding "Will Work for Food" signs at busy intersections. You can't help every single person, but it's inhuman to pretend not to see them each and every time you hit a stoplight. I know many kind people who just don't feel right about giving money to the homeless, worrying that they may be paying for an alcohol addiction or their next drug fix. But the truly compassionate still find a way to give. I know of one elderly lady who has begun collecting coupons or gift certificates for free meals at local restaurants. She keeps them in the ashtray of her car, and is happy to pass them along to the hungry. Once, my sister, who was sixteen at the time, was moved to tears by the sight of a small family on the street corner with a sign that read, simply, "hungry." She had no cash on her, but told the family to wait five minutes. She sped home and made peanut-butter-and-jelly sand-wiches out of an entire loaf of bread, shoved the sandwiches back into the bread sack, and returned to the family. Tears were shed on their end, too.

BE KIND

If you have a chance to interact with the needy, make a point to talk to them like you would any individual—your neighbor, a business associate, a family mem-ber. Often, there's no better gift than the feeling of worth and civilization they feel when someone treats them like a real person. I once read a newspaper fea-ture on the homeless, in which one of the individuals profiled said something I'll always remember: "You don't think I feel like crap when a generous person takes me into a restaurant and feeds me? Here I am in the clothes I wore yes-terday and smelling like trash. But you can take my mind off that by speaking nicely to me and not looking down on me."

The poor aren't just looking for money. They're looking for understanding, sig-nificance, a human connection—gifts to which no dollar amount applies.

THEY'RE LOOKING FOR UNDERSTANDING, SIGNIFICANCE, A HUMAN CONNECTION— GIFTS TO WHICH NO DOLLAR AMOUNT APPLIES.

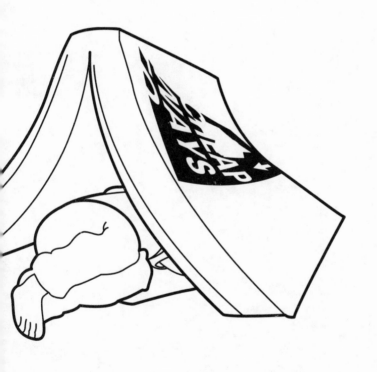

PERSONAL IMPROVEMENT

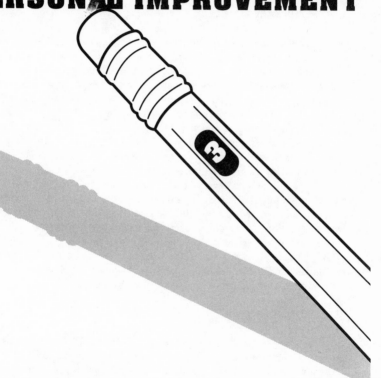

CHEAP WAYS TO BUY CLOTHES

By Margaret Feinberg

When it comes to clothes, the four-letter word "sale" is still the best. Along with it, there's an entire family of friendly vernacular including, "liquidation," "clearance," "going out of business," "marked down," and "reduced." For the savvy shopper, there are always ways to avoid paying full retail.

KNOW THE SALES CYCLE

Visit your favorite stores and talk to sales clerks and managers about their store's markdown process. Most stores have a policy established for how their items progress from full retail to reduced price. It may be based on when new shipments are scheduled to arrive, how quickly the majority of sizes in a style sell through, or the number of weeks (or even days) clothes are on display.

Be friendly to sales people and ask them about upcoming sales. Does the store have annual or seasonal sales? How often do markdowns occur? Are products generally marked down in the morning, evening, or on particular days of the week? One major chain is known to move items to the sale rack on Mondays, making that one of the best days to shop for savings and selection. Knowing how the system works will help you determine whether you should go ahead and pay full retail for an item or wait an extra week for significant savings.

Always keep your receipts and study the return policies. Some clothing stores have no-questions-asked return policies for one to three months. Take advantage of them. You never know when a shirt is going to shrink or a button is going to fall off. The receipt can also help if you decide on a must-have piece of clothing one week and find it marked down the next. Many stores will honor the new reduced price if you can prove your purchase with a receipt.

BEELINE TO THE BACK

Where you shop in a store can also play into the final total. Experienced shoppers know that the real bargains on clothes are found on the racks at the back of the store and will make an appropriate beeline to this area when shopping. Some stores will entice shoppers with sale racks toward the front of the store, but the majority of price reductions will almost always be found in the back. Most of these racks will be filled with post-seasonal wear. Take advantage of the

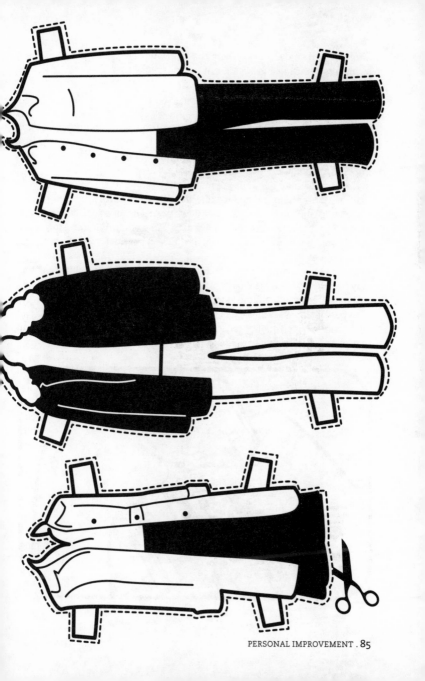

bargains and enjoy wearing them the following year. As a general rule, buy swimsuits in the fall and sweaters in the spring.

WHEN TO PAY MORE

It's also important to know what's important to you in clothing so you can determine when it's worthwhile to pay more. How important is style? How important is being trendy? How important is wearing a name brand? How important is quality?

Know which name brands are important to you and which of your items really need to be name brands. A name brand pair of jeans or jacket will be used for years to come, while a white T-shirt usually needs to be replaced regularly. Remember that your basics don't have to be name brand. Without a logo, most people won't know whether you bought your socks at Abercrombie or at a sock factory outlet store.

Invest in pieces that offer durability, quality, and longevity. White tank tops may come and go, but great pairs of jeans, leather belts, khaki pants, and black jackets will be around for the long haul.

Hyper-trendiness can get expensive. Remember that extremely trendy pieces don't have to be top quality, especially if you can already tell they'll be "in" this season and "out" the next.

STEPPING OUTSIDE THE MALL

If you're going to save money on clothes, sooner or later you're going to have to shop someplace other than the mall. But before you go too far, visit less popular, out of the way malls. Those aged, unattractive malls often contain great finds. Because of the lower foot traffic, higher quality products usually make it to the sales racks.

Many find refuge in factory outlet stores springing up all across the country. While factory outlets can offer great savings and sales, they're not always your best bet. Little known fact: some major name brand clothing manufacturers actually make lower quality products specifically for their factory outlet stores. So you're not always getting the same quality for less. The buyers also vary from store to store, so a name brand store in one town may have better quality and selection of product than in another.

ON CONSIGNMENT

Another alternative is consignment shops. Since these are independently owned, the quality and styles of the clothing accepted varies greatly. When visiting, note the clothing available, but also keep an eye on the owner. People have a natural tendency to stock what they like and wear themselves. If you want hip, young clothing, try to find a consignment shop run by a younger person. If you're looking for more mature wear, shop at stores run by elderly management.

Even if you can't find anything you like at a consignment shop, consider selling your old clothes at one. Research individual store's policies for the percentages they keep and any stocking fees. Use the money you make to buy new clothing.

If your clothes are too dated to be accepted by a consignment shop but are still in decent condition, donate them to a local charity and enjoy the tax write-off.

THRIFTY ALTERNATIVES

Thrift stores such as Goodwill and the Salvation Army also offer a wide variety of clothes for reasonable prices. It may take a bit of hunting, but there are usually deals and quality pieces to be had. Consider volunteering your time to sort clothes at one of these establishments in exchange for first pick and reduced prices.

Garage sales, yard sales, and rummage sales can contain some treasures, and most of the prices are negotiable. If you're not willing to sort through the out-of-date, worn, and stained piles of clothing, consider working with friends to freshen up your closet. Agree to trade pieces from time to time with those who are about the same size.

SWAP IT ALL

For a more permanent exchange, consider organizing a clothes swap. This can be done among a small group of friends. Invite them to bring a certain number of items, cleaned and on hangers with the size clearly displayed. Throw a party where you exchange clothes.

Or organize a larger clothes swap as a fundraiser. Invite people to donate clothes. Organize into styles and sizes. Charge everyone five dollars a bag for the clothes they select. Those who help organize the event get first pick. Donate the money to a local service group, mission, or church.

OH YEAH, AND...

Other ways to save money on clothes don't include shopping at all. In order to maintain the clothes you have, don't buy harsh detergents. Hang to dry rather than use the dryer. Invest in good spot removers. And try to maintain your weight. Serious weight fluctuations require you to buy more clothing to adapt to your changing body.

CHEAP WAYS TO LOOK CHEAP-CHIC

By KATIE MEIER

When disheveled became more a look than an insult in the modern world, people strove to find ways to imitate the laid back style sported by their favorite stars. From the reclassification of T-shirts and sneaks to cool, to a reconfiguration of style that now transcends gender, age, and bank balance, the search for the cheap-chic is on; the trick is to get it for less.

Without a doubt the first rule of cheap-chic is attitude; and that can be had for free. Part of dressing cheap-chic is acting like cheap is chic. Too often chic is understood as the domain of those with money to spend. As a friend who spent years on Hollywood sets as an extra always says: chic only looks that way because stylists, stars, and others act like it is, not because they spent money to make it so.

However attitude won't be nearly enough if you're going for the cheap-chic; that is unless you live someplace that takes kindly to the "nude-attitude." If you don't find yourself so fortunate, the first place to head is the thrift store for some clothes. There you'll find a mixture of old and new that you can combine to change as easily as every season's trends.

THRIFT TIP NUMBER ONE

Surprisingly, thrift doesn't always mean cheap. With the transformation of cool moving from glam to the shabby ne'er-do-well, costs have increased in the land of thrift. To assure you're getting actual thrift prices, stay clear of stores specializing in "recycled" fashions. These stores usually mix thrift with full cost items, and market their clothing somewhere in between. Instead, look for thrift organizations that have been around for years. These companies often have larger clearinghouse centers for their organizations in urban cities, in addition to local branches scattered throughout the grid.

THRIFT TIP NUMBER TWO

Not all neighborhoods are created equal. Thrift tends to fluctuate with the neighborhoods in which it's featured, so you'll want to reverse conventional wisdom here and head away from the high class. For example, the same pair of

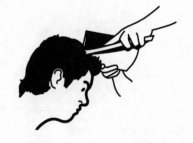

old-school slacks—the core component of many a cheap-chic wardrobe—can range in price from one dollar to ten dollars. When you're going for chic, a ten-spot might seem a pittance, but here we're going for chic and cheap. Get used to an adjusted price scale in the world of thrift; ten bucks for pants simply won't do.

Beyond getting chic through thrift, deals abound in the commercial market as well. To look great for less, get with the children's department or "baby" and "kids" versions of your favorite stores. And, though outlets should be placed in the annuls of cheap-history, there are still deals to be had if you know what type of outlet to look for. Here's the scoop on these suggestions:

TOTS AND TEES, BOYS AND GIRLS

Not to take advantage of the rising waistlines of today's tots, but sizes sold for kids in their pre-teens often fit full-grown adults. The cheap equation here: Stores sell the same items at different prices depending on which department, or even branch of a store, the items appear. Because many items feature size charts complete with measurements, it will be easy to assure yourself how close in size to a twelve-year-old you really are. If you're still not sure, get old school about it and get to the dressing room; it might not fit, but to save big on the same item why not try? And, if you're a woman, try walking over to the men's department. Boys have been secretly saving—by comparison—on items like socks, tees, and jeans for years.

TAKE THE CHIC, CHEAP

Commercial cheap-chic can also be found in the world of outlet malls. Be wary here though, as outlet is no longer a synonym for deal, but instead for daytrip. Collections of commercial retailers are never as cheap as single outlet stores to which these retailers send their last-seasons. For those who happen to live near a store, cheap-chic can be had by buying the chic, cheap. From post-season Prada, to other brand names in overstock, cheap-chic can become a bit higher class in these bargain shopping stores. Call your favorite retailer to find where these bargains lie; a daytrip to the outlets will pale in comparison.

Of course, getting a look together doesn't stop with the clothes. No outfit is complete in the world of cheap-chic without that "just out of bed and proud of it" hair. From boys who wear it whacked-out, to girls who want to look two-days post wash, hair is an essential component of a crafted look. Here's how to get tailored tresses without a ton of cash:

TRESSES TIP NUMBER ONE

Taper your edges. This quick, cheap, and easy clip can create the cheap-chic look in seconds flat. For the cost of some shears from the beauty supply store, you can skip the salon that charges a bundle to make a mess of your ends. Simply hold the shears vertical and snip at the tips of your ends. This quick trick creates a cheap-chic edge, just like the full-price pros.

TRESSES TIP NUMBER TWO

Make your own morning hair. Just as the "wet-look" means we're not actually soaked, the "morning look" means we're going faux as well; the best morning hair is made. But leave pricey "Bedhead" products alone, as fifties style pomade works just fine and is as cheap as the place they sell it—the dime store.

TRESSES TIP NUMBER THREE

Combine color with kitchenware. Your home is now a safe place to get colored on the cheap, provided you keep the color simple. Madonna has no place in the home, so keep to a smaller task—say, highlights—and you can skip the salon. From boxes of blonde to any color under the sun, coloring comes cheap when it comes from the drugstore and combines with your kitchen. Just a simple whip, bang, mix of the box ingredients, combined with a basting brush and some foil can add up to a cheap way to get the shine you desire. Simply cut the foil in to sections, and use each one to keep highlights apart. Put the hair to be colored flat on the foil, brush with color, and fold all sides of the foil in. The color stays neat, and you keep the job cheap.

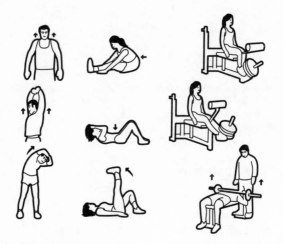

CHEAP WAYS TO EXERCISE

By Jason Boyett

As a student, you probably got a lot of exercise in college, from walking on campus to enjoying the benefits of a free pass to the campus fitness center. Then graduation came, bringing with it a diploma and taking with it a cheap fitness regimen. And being a poor and possibly married ex-student with meager job options, you probably aren't about to pay thirty bucks a month or four hundred dollars a year to join a bunch of muscle heads at the nearby gym. But you don't have to join a high-priced gym or buy the newest Ab Flab Master in three easy installments to stay in good shape. Exercise is cheap. All you need is a willing body and a little discipline. Here's how to keep the muscles toned and the calories burning on a low budget:

GET OUTSIDE

Once the weather gets warm, there's no excuse to hang around indoors. Have you ever noticed how people will get in their car to drive a mile or two to the gym—where they promptly climb onto a treadmill and start walking or jogging? Why not just cut out the fancy equipment and expensive memberships and walk to the park? Or jog a few times around the block? Plenty of parks have jogging trails that help you keep track of how far you've gone. If you prefer to stay in the neighborhood, use your car's odometer to determine a distance—say, three-quarters of a mile from where you live. Then jog or walk to that point, turn around, and head back home. Do it every other day, or alternate jogging and walking from day-to-day. The idea is to get your heart rate going and work off the calories. And on that note, remember this: Some outdoor activities like gardening can burn as many calories (ninety calories after fifteen minutes) as more conventional exercise activities (water aerobics: seventy after fifteen minutes).

DEFY CONVENIENCE

This involves changing the all-American mindset that glorifies the quick and easy. Convenience is for lazy people.

Lesson One: Stay off the elevator. Instead of riding the elevator at work or in your apartment building, use the stairs. There's a reason stair-climbing machines are popular—walking up the stairs is good exercise. Find a well-maintained and safely lit flight of stairs and frequent it.

Lesson Two: Nearby parking is for sissies. By the time you've circled the Wal-Mart parking lot three times looking for the closest space, you could have parked way out on the perimeter and walked to the door already—all the while benefiting from some excellent activity. Next time you're at the movie theater or the mall or the grocery store, forget waiting for the old lady in the Cadillac to ease her boat into the traffic flow. Park as far away as you can and cover the distance at a brisk walking pace. No one else will be out there, so at the least you'll get fewer door dings.

STAY AT HOME

Is kickboxing in a class of twenty at the gym any better for you than doing the same thing at home? Not really. The one disadvantage of solitary exercise is the need for greater discipline—it's much easier to give up and rest when no one's watching than it is when you're surrounded by pretty girls or sweaty guys. But the activity? No difference. From "Abs of Steel" to "Xtreme Strength Training," there's an exercise video available for every specialty. But here's the trick: Don't buy one unless you're sure you like the program and regimen. (How many dusty, unused "Buns of Steel" videos are currently sitting in American closets?) Take one for a test drive by renting it first from your favorite video store, or check it out from the library. Once you've decided on a program, look around. Refuse to buy the video brand new. Check out garage sales, eBay, the discount rack at Best Buy. Exercise videos are as faddish as anything else (Tae-Bo, anyone?), and once the fad wears out its welcome, you can usually find the tapes for cheap.

Note: Exercise videos exist for almost any kind of toning or workout you can think of. Not all are equal. Before you start, check out the following for reviews and recommendations: *www.exercisevideosreviews.com*; *www.videofitness.com*

FINAL TIP

One big advantage of gym memberships, besides the ubiquitous mirrors and tanning products, is the motivation factor. Personal trainers, convenient equipment, and fellow enthusiasts do a lot to help you maintain focus and intensity. It's harder on your own. A good idea if you're staying at home is to keep a personal workout log. Track whatever you want—activity, mileage, heart rate, calories burned—as long as you record something from every workout. Success motivates. Keep at it, and there's no reason you can't stay in great shape without thinning your wallet.

CHEAP WAYS TO DEVELOP A LIBRARY
By Jason Boyett (with Faith Hopler)

As a former English major and a writer, I have a weakness: books. I love the way they feel, their weight in my hand. I love the smell of old, crisp paper, the creak of the binding when you crack open a hardback. I like the idea of a pocket-sized book like this one, that you can carry anywhere. I admire a good row of books on a shelf, arranged alphabetically by author, or by subject, or by category, or just by the way their spines look next to each other. I think books are very, very cool. Yes, my wife thinks I'm a dork, too.

When I enter someone's house, the first thing I look for is his or her bookshelf. Upon finding it, I spend time there, perusing the titles. What do my hosts consider their "top-shelf" titles? How are the books arranged? If the eyes are a window to the soul, then a person's bookshelf must be a window to their mind. Should I happen upon a home with few books to be seen, I say a prayer for its occupants. I confess to being a book snob.

I'm not much of one for traditional collections, but I guess you could say I have always collected books: fiction, non-fiction, biographies, theology, classics, and contemporary best sellers. The first thing I set out to do when I moved into my own place was to develop a good personal library of books—for reference, for pleasure, for decoration, whatever. One problem: New books can be expensive. A modest bookshelf may measure three feet long. You can probably fit eight or so books of average length within a linear foot. A brand-new hardback will cost you twenty dollars at the very least. Add it up. That's $480, just to fill one shelf. Yikes.

There's a better way. Since books are relatively timeless, you can get just as much out of a used one as a pristine, never-been-opened one. Most of the books in my library have come to me second-hand. Here's how to stock up on books, appear well-read, and feed your mind without going into debt.

THRIFT STORES

In addition to ratty couches, clothing from the Reagan administration, and mismatched dishware, people donate lots of books to charities like Goodwill, Volunteers of America, and the Salvation Army. Check out their thrift stores. Often, you'll only find old copies of *Cosmo*, laughably dated titles like FORTRAN *for Beginners*, and a glut of Harlequin romance novels. Sometimes, though, you'll find a gem. I got a clean, barely read pocket paperback of *Lonesome Dove* once at Goodwill. It was next to a stack of nice hardback classics for a dollar apiece— and every library needs a few works by Dickens, Melville, or Twain. Without fail, you'll also find some cheap Reader's Digest Condensed books. I don't usually like to read those, but they do fill up shelf space if you want books for decorative purposes.

FLEA MARKETS

Based on my experience, flea markets in big cities contain a lot of antiques. Flea markets in small- to mid-sized cities like mine contain a lot of useless crap. And chickens and rabbits. And funnel cakes, if you get there early enough on Saturday. But if you look carefully, there's generally a bookstall to be found at even the smallest flea market. Most likely you'll find loads of last year's bestselling paperbacks. Sometimes you'll encounter a treasure. A friend once gave me a leather-bound soft cover 1889 edition of *The Imitation of Christ* by Thomas à Kempis, one of Christianity's most influential early devotional writers. It's a beautiful book, and in great shape. It was discovered at a flea market, and picked up for a couple of bucks.

USED BOOKSTORES

There are all kinds of used bookstores, with all kinds of books. Some stock only used college textbooks. Some sell rare first editions. Others may specialize in fantasy, romance, westerns, or science fiction. More often, used bookstores are carving out a niche market, as former independent bookstore owners are finding that's the only way they can survive in a Barnes & Noble-saturated world. Still, a used bookstore with depth and decent prices can be a recreational destination. It's worth the time to find a good one, especially one that can support a couple of hours of browsing, with prices low enough to let you take a risk on something you haven't read yet.

One cool thing about used bookstores is the possibility of trade-ins. One store I frequent offers "one paperback free when you bring in three." Over the years, I've accumulated some books I have no interest in keeping. A few weeks ago, I traded three of them in for a nice copy of the seminal sci-fi/fantasy, *Ender's Game*, by Orson Scott Card. Three books I had no use for got me one book I really wanted, one I intended to keep. Good deal.

A decent used bookstore chain to consider is Half Price Books. They're spread throughout the Midwest and West Coast, so if you live near one you should get acquainted. Half Price has the bulk rate advantage of a chain store, blended with the ethos and community spirit of a local shop. They've got a pretty comprehensive selection of new hardbacks (which average around seven dollars) and tons of paperbacks. Check out the clearance section—shelves of books at twenty-five or fifty cents a pop. Heaven for book lovers.

LIBRARY SALES

My favorite weekend of the year occurs annually every June. It's the "Friends of the Library" book sale held in the basement of my city's downtown library. Prior to the event, library patrons donate books to be sold for the library's benefit. The library system joins the fun itself, using the book sale as a way to reduce circulation and control inventory. The result is shelf upon shelf of quality books for outlandishly cheap prices. I'd wager that one-quarter of the books I own came from these library sales over the years. That's maybe sixty or seventy books, from year-old Stephen King novels to theological works from the 1960s, for which I probably paid a grand sum of fifteen dollars—total.

Library sales typically occur in two stages. The first stage brings in the most money, as the better titles are purchased for two or three dollars each. Then, stage two kicks in—sometimes in the second day of the sale, sometimes a week or month later. The purpose of stage two is just to get rid of what's left. At this point, my library offers books for a dollar a bag. They'll give you a paper grocery bag at the door. You fill it up and pay them a dollar on the way out.

The good thing is, these sales are often so haphazard that you're bound to find some great books during stage two—like the first edition hardback of John Irving's *A Prayer for Owen Meany* I pulled off a shelf several years back. I basically accumulated every volume of Henri Nouwen's devotional writings at a succession of library sales, spending less than the price of a hamburger on the whole set. Ask around about library book sales in your community. You can build up your personal collection in a hurry, and support your local library at the same time.

And finally, don't forget to check two additional places. From *Half.com* to *BookCloseOuts.com* to eBay and Amazon, there are plenty of cheap books to be found at reasonable prices online. And secondly, make a habit of browsing the clearance section at Barnes & Noble or Borders. You can almost always find remainders (titles that failed to sell) priced far below their original worth. Happy book hunting. Just don't forget to read.

CHEAP WAYS TO STAY EDUCATED

By Katie Meier

Remember back in the day when college costs barely topped two thousand dollars for the entire year? Nope, me neither. But my Dad keeps this memory on the front burner in our house because ... well, I'm not sure why. As unhelpful as his reminiscence about ten cent cheeseburgers or homes that cost under fifty thousand dollars can be, his comments do in fact impress upon the younger generation one simple fact: things cost these days. And because they do, choices have to be made. But abandoning the life of learning need not be one of them. If you follow these simple steps to getting education on the cheap, you can get it forever.

USE THE NET

For those who slept through "A European History of One-Handed Potato Famine Farmers" in college, fear not; the course is on the net and you can get crackin' by taking it again. In fact, you can take nearly every course you snoozed through, couldn't squeeze in under attendance restrictions, hoped to take, or weren't far enough along in coursework to tackle.

The web is the cheapest way toward competency in all manner of coursework as course syllabi are abundant across the Internet. To get these classes on the cheap, simply find a course you'd like to take by surfing the department website at any college, find the required reading list or syllabus, buy the materials, then follow along with course readings and assignments as listed on the site. Some classes also feature chat, message boards, or other forms of information and discussion for the course, all accessible for free.

Total cost? Zero, if you're of the strength to withstand hours in the local library. There, Internet is free and so are the books necessary to take many courses found online. If you're more the "do-they-even-still-make-libraries?" type, total cost to you is simply the fee for home Internet service and the cash put out to buy the books; that is, if you can't find them online, free. No, it's not too good to be true—free books abound on the Internet, no stealing required. Many Classics, poetry, or English courses require old-school books that have lost their copyrights and are now fair game as they're "public domain." From Homer's *Odyssey* to Mark Twain's *Huck Finn*, these texts are free to you, provided you get up the gumption to hunt them down.

EDUCATION AND BOOKSTORES DON'T GO HAND IN HAND

The wisest in the world know online is the better place for education through books. The wisdom of this statement is so profound, it's likely Mr. Miyagi taught it to Karate Kid, right after "paint the fence." To get the cheapest deals, find the books needed using a price "farming," or comparison-shopping site. Note which bookstore features the best deals, overall, as you'll want to order all books from the same site, saving money on shipping in the end. Next, walk your www. way over to "deal" catcher, or coupon sites to see who's offering what. From free shipping to twenty, forty, or even fifty dollars off, get with the coupon that gives you the most savings. Combine the coupon with the lowest priced store, and presto, you can kiss the strip-mall goodbye.

But be advised, cheap is as cheap does and those who do it cheap order big. Initial standard shipping will run a couple bucks each order, with other books coming in at only pennies on the dollar, so order once to get away from paying the initial shipping fee again and again.

CRASH A LECTURE OR CONFERENCE

"Crash" is such a negative word; it just seems so darn intrusive. But as this book seeks to go the gusto with connotations, like "cheap," that seem negative to some, I second this motion and advocate that "crash" is yet another word that should lose its stigma.

We're not talking party crashing here, no disruptions or drunken diving off the neighbor's roof are required. Nope, just good old sitting-in on talks, demonstrations, or discussions about topics that interest you. Each year cities feature any number of conventions, convocations, lecture series, and lengthy national meetings of this or that Association of America. From religion to science, to computers to toys, to baking, art, and law, to those who love to pretend the world is still medieval, you can join the discussion, and often for free. Simply check the schedule of various hotels or conference centers in your city to see who'll be swinging by.

Academics are a cheap bunch—just the way we like 'em—and will often let you in their conferences for little over ten or twenty bucks. Of course, seminars or workshops are a different story, so stay clear of these "weekend-oriented" events where the speakers expect big cash and look to boot those who haven't coughed it up.

In addition, don't forget to seek out speaker series' at your local library, college, or museum. There, the price tag to partake in discussion will likely rival that of the coffee you'll be sipping as you bask in the glow of cheap knowledge.

GET CRAFTY, HANDY, OR ANY OTHER "Y"

Often we limit our view of education to the world of burgundy-lined libraries complete with leather bound books. However, thinking beyond the box here can satisfy the desire to get creativity as a side dish with education on the cheap.

Handy-style superstores offer a bevy of learning experiences, ranging in cost from free to the simple price of the project itself. Want to learn to lay wood flooring, make a mosaic patio table, or get as fancy with faux painting as the next guy? Then take the weekend-warrior route and get enrolled at your local hardware store for one of their "demo" classes. The same goes for those who hope to be crafty, artsy, or musical; okay, the latter perhaps is a stretch, but the same concept applies. Education on the cheap begins by taking advantage of the demonstrations sponsored by specific stores. And because the opportunities for learning rival only the square-footage of some of these stores, avenues for education are endless.

SAY IT TO YOURSELF AND MEAN IT … "TV IS GOOD!"

When the couch is calling your name, embrace the remote control with love and find education on the tube. After all, it's cheap and informative, parking is a breeze, and dress is optional. Try individual cable channels specializing in history, art, science, animals, or the environment. Or try local public broadcasting stations for televised courses, lectures, or discussions.

CHEAP WAYS TO GET PUBLISHED

By Margaret Feinberg

Whether it's a story, idea, or recipe collection, finding a publisher for it is becoming more difficult. Traditional publishers are bombarded with thousands of manuscripts each year and only publish a few hundred (or even dozen) each year. Very few are from first-time authors. So how do you get your ideas published?

FOCUS, FOCUS, FOCUS

You need to reflect on what you're trying to accomplish with your writing to determine which route is the most cost effective. Are you publishing a collection of recipes or a genealogy of your family members? Is this an autobiography or testimonial? Are you trying to establish yourself as a writer? Do you plan on selling it or giving it away?

GOOD OLE COPY SHOP

Depending on the size and scope the project, your local office supply store may be the place to start. Many offer services including photocopying and binding at reasonable prices. If you're trying to cut corners, buy the paper and binders in bulk separately, make the photocopies yourself and put the manuals or booklets together on your own. Try to avoid copying pages on your home-based computer printer, where costs for ink cartridges can soar.

HOLD THE PAPER

To skip the paper process completely, consider posting all or a portion of your work on the Internet using your own website. The Internet is the quickest, easiest way to get your ideas published. Most servers offer free web pages to members that allow you to display your photos, thoughts, wisdom, stories, plans, and advice. Also consider pitching your story or ideas to already-established websites looking to expand their content. If you're actually looking to publish—meaning print—your ideas, then it's going to take a little more planning.

PUBLISHING REALITY CHECK

If you're looking for a traditional publisher, you're going to need to put together a book proposal, which includes information about the author, a market analysis, an outline sample chapter, and a marketing plan. In short, you need to create something that will sell.

Traditional publishers are extremely selective and most won't even consider unsolicited manuscripts, preferring to work with established authors and agents. Traditional publishers purchase the manuscript from the author and handle all costs related to the book including printing, marketing, distribution, and design. The publisher takes all the financial risk. The author does not pay for anything, but grants a variety of rights for which he or she receives a portion of the sales in the form of royalties, usually ranging from 8 to 15 percent based on either the full retail or wholesale costs of the book.

THE DO-IT YOURSELF PUBLISHING WORLD

If you have a book idea you want to publish and haven't found a book publisher, self-publishing may be the way to go. A number of companies provide these services, and their ads can be found online and in the back of writing magazines. There are different forms of self-publishing. Before you settle up with one company, here are a few things you should know about each.

A subsidy publisher is selective about the manuscripts they consider, but unlike traditional publishers, they ask the author to pay for a portion of the publication costs. Subsidy publishers provide services such as editing, marketing, distribution, and warehousing, but still keep most, if not all, of the rights. Like traditional publishers, authors receive payment based on royalties.

A vanity publisher is not selective and prints the book at the author's full expense. Vanity publishers may offer pre-packaged services such as editing, marketing, and promotional services for an additional fee. The author retains rights and all profits from the sales.

Self-publishing is a lot like vanity publishing in that the author is responsible for the entire publication, including marketing, distribution, and storage, but the author has the option to bid out every aspect of the process and this can become more cost-effective than vanity publishing. If done properly, it can result in a better quality product. With self-publishing the writer maintains all rights and keeps all of the profits.

Print-on-demand companies offer digital subsidy publishing services. The books are stored on a computer disk and printed as they are ordered. The cost is far less for the author, since books are only produced as needed, and the process ensures you don't end up with thousands of dollars tied up in unused or unsold books in the garage or attic. Print-on-demand works best for orders of books under a few hundred.

E-ALTERNATIVE

E-books are a new technology that allows your book to be read on a computer screen or handheld device. E-books currently exist in several formats but are still struggling to find widespread readership. A book can be released as an e-book for as little as a few hundred dollars.

KEEP IN MIND

The cost of subsidy and vanity publishing can be significant, because these companies usually have significant minimum orders (five hundred to one thousand) and charge accordingly to ensure a profit margin. These types of publishers have gotten a bad rap over the years due to some companies participating in fraudulent and unethical behavior. Before signing any contracts, examine other books the publisher has produced for quality. Request references. Get all promises, including the final price, in print in the contract, and talk to other writers who have self-published for recommendations.

If your goal is to get your work published and establish yourself as a writer, you need to be aware of the reputation of non-traditional publishers. Vanity, subsidy, and self-publishers have a stigma, because authors who have to pay to get published are not taken seriously in the publishing world. Many publications won't even consider reviewing a book published in this way, and it can be difficult to convince bookstores to stock your book. There are exceptions, including *What Color Is Your Parachute?*, *The Christmas Box*, and *The Celestine Prophecy*, that prove that self-publishing can be successful venture.

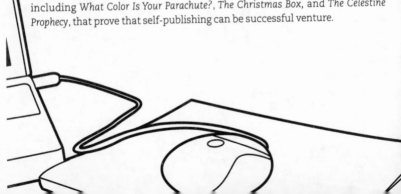

CHEAP WAYS TO GET A BACHELOR'S DEGREE By Katie Meier

If you're looking ahead to college and a bachelor's degree, here's advice on how to speed ahead at significantly reduced rates. From where you choose to do your general education, to the type of grades you elect to earn, a bachelor's degree can cost anywhere from a few hundred dollars to tens of thousands. Here's the lowdown on keeping costs cheap.

GETTING STARTED

It's not fashionable, and no one will peg you as the brainiac you might truly be, but you should do it anyway—choose community college.

General education requirements, those courses completed in your first two years of college, are roughly transferable anywhere provided you're attending an accredited institution. You can take English 101 at a private school for hundreds of dollars per unit, or you can show off your smarts by taking the course from your local junior college (JC) for somewhere between ten and fifty dollars per unit.

Magically, this formula applies to English as well as nearly all classes you'll take as a freshman or sophomore. The nine to twelve units you'll pay for each semester become a walk in the park at, say, twenty bucks a unit, while strain, despair, and large-scale loans will ensue when you plan to go private, paying upwards of three hundred dollars per unit. Ouch! That's nine-hundy for just one class. Even state schools can't beat the rate your community college offers. If you're bound to tackle the same subjects why not do it on the cheap?

Once vanity is cast aside and you're sold on the JC experience, scholarship opportunities abound. The reason: flat-out flakiness. You'll find many at the JC who, to be nice, are what's known as "on the circuit," cruising from JC to JC, course to course. This flaky attitude is a boon to those looking for free money and cheap education. After all, it takes time, effort, and determination to track free money down in the student services office. The result for you? A good chunk of your fellow JC classmates can be counted out in the race to compete for free funds.

Additionally, community colleges increase your chance of winning free funds because they enroll fewer students than big four-year schools. Fewer students, means fewer scholarship applicants, means less competition in the pools for free money. And, with the lower cost of JC education, you needn't worry if you can't land that million-dollar scholarship deal. The little grant you can win from the local gardner's association will likely cover the cost of your fees; at JC, a little goes a long way.

GROWING OUT

As you work your way toward freshman and sophomore requirements at your local JC, look for something called reciprocity agreements. Sometimes these agreements have different names—check with a counselor at your college—but all seek to shine favor on local, hardworking community college students like yourself.

In plain speak, a reciprocity agreement basically makes students this amazing promise: I, (insert name of really great four-year school), promise to admit, (insert your name), provided he/she finishes the following list of classes with this or that particular GPA. It's that simple. You can skip the cost of freshman and sophomore year at the big four-year, and still count on getting in two years later, as a junior. Reciprocity agreements are some of the best relationships students will ever be in: expectations are out on the table, both parties declare their undying love for one another, and the agreement means big four-years can't break up with students even if they want to—so there.

Applying to a four-year as a JC transfer student—whether you've pursued reciprocity or not—has additional benefits. You're now in a considerably smaller pool of applicants, one restricted to "transfer" status, skipping past all those high school seniors seeking freshman entry along with every other Joe, Dick, or Sally off the street. Again, smaller application pools mean less competition to win free money. Some bang up grades at community college paired with a decreased pool of applicants can easily translate into a full ride at the four year. Do everything you can while at junior college to polish your academic veneer to a high gloss shine; join the honors institute, take accelerated courses, work on independent research or join with a professor to do fieldwork.

GETTING MORE

When you get there, most four-years have a wealth of on-campus opportunities for you to win free funds. Two of the best, and least researched, resources are departmental research positions and the school's alumni association(s). Here's how to navigate these systems.

Research positions are usually posted near department offices. They'll likely look like a hefty, hanging phone book warding away all those too timid to take the time to read this apparent behemoth. This works to your benefit then, as few individuals make it all the way through the book and even fewer walk themselves to the office, request the correct forms, return them by the deadline, and follow up on their application.

If assigned a research position, you'll be paid in cash, which you can then use to cover tuition expenses. In addition, you'll receive research experience you can add to your academic resume. Graduate school comes cheaper to those who can win scholarships and grants by showing how they shined as undergraduates.

Alumni associations are also a great place to score free funds. These associations are collectives of ex-students who love their Alma Mater so much they choose to plug money back into the school and into students who are just like they used to be—undergrads working toward a degree. These associations look for applicants who do interesting things with their free time, from dabbling in the arts, to service work abroad, to community based involvement, and more. Competition isn't as fierce as you might imagine, either. Alumni associations often come up short on student applicants, leaving funds undistributed for the year. So, get yourself to the alumni association at your school and see what they require. The money offered is free; no strings attached.

CHEAP WAYS TO GET A MASTER'S DEGREE

By Katie Meier

After you've jettisoned the world of undergrad education, your thrill might turn to shrill as you consider the costs of an advanced degree. Private programs can run nearly thirty thousand dollars per year, leaving you in debt to the tune of sixty thousand dollars for a two-year degree like an MA. However, there are ways to defer these costs, and we're not talking about hokey scholarships for left-handed-children-of-divorce-from-Armenia-who-long-to-study-French-literature. Rather, we're talking real cash, direct from your school or graduate program to you.

GETTING STARTED

The first thing to do if you're looking to curb the cost of education is offer to kick something back; apply as a graduate assistant, also know as a TA or RA, in your department.

TA: A teaching assistant's job takes them into the heart of undergrad education. TAs help facilitate lectures, run discussion/section, prepare course materials, and most importantly, TAs grade, grade, grade. TAs are expected to hold office hours each week in order to assist undergrads along the way.

RA: Research assistants report to faculty members working on particular projects. Most often, RAs help compile, catalogue, and compartmentalize information; can you say L-I-B-R-A-R-Y or L-A-B? Cause this is where RAs spend the majority of time. RAs meet with faculty advisors independently and are not usually expected to set firm office hours.

Here's the skinny on tuition breaks when you work as a TA/RA. These jobs come in something called appointments, usually from one-fourth or one-third time to half time. It's a simple equation: the greater the appointment, the greater the tuition break. Not all appointments waive 100 percent of tuition, but they all have the potential to waive some. And, let's all say it together, "Some money from our school is less money from our pocket!" Every penny counts.

An added benefit: Those who win TA/RAships get paid. Stipends are paid out to students directly but can be applied to any tuition or fees a TA/RAship does not cover, further decreasing the burden of tuition.

GOING ABOUT GETTING IT CHEAP

• Read the paperwork. Many people don't realize TA/RA positions exist until they've applied, enrolled, and paid full-boat for the first year of graduate education.

• Document your meteoric rise to academic stardom by sending top-tier transcripts. Most schools require at least a 3.0 for TA/RAships, and expect you to keep this GPA while completing six hours each term.

• Document your notoriously magnanimous character and spirit of enthusiasm for learning and education. Here I'm talking about a bang-up essay and recommendations that rate. Also include those extracurriculars and academic achievements related to your field of study.

• Be the super-star who actually completes and returns all paperwork by the appropriate deadlines; people who complete the paperwork staff TA/RA appointments. You need good grades, a good essay, a "shiny" façade, and some good recommendations, but you also need to get them in on time.

ON YOUR MIND WHEN IN HOT PURSUIT

Consult the school you plan to attend for specifics. Different departments have higher and lower stipend rates for TA/RAs. If you're in the sciences get ready to make some serious cash (well, at least compared to your fellow TA/RA studying romance languages in the literature department).

Programs pay for your prior experience. A Ph.D. program will pay more than an MA program.

Schools pay more for "shiny buttons." Most graduate programs want to know what you'll contribute to their department. Got mad organization skills? Already have teaching experience? Been published? Spoke at conferences? Already built a working bridge for the Department of Transportation? It all counts, especially when applying to competitive programs like psychology, English, or engineering.

More free money doesn't necessarily translate into the cheapest education. A TA/RAship that pays $18,000 at one school might be a less lucrative offer than an appointment paying $12,000 at a school located somewhere less expensive to live. Also, put tuition first. If you can swing a TA/RAship that waives all tuition, the deal is significantly sweeter than one offering you a bigger stipend but no tuition assistance. Getting school on the cheap translates to getting tuition at the lowest cost.

HOME
IMPR

CHEAP WAYS TO GIVE A ROOM
A FACELIFT By Jason Boyett

After four years of marriage and apartment living, my wife and I were ready to buy our first home. Taking the plunge, we eventually found a house in a quiet neighborhood, with a big yard and an inviting floor plan. It was perfect, except for a few minor details of taste—the salmon-colored kitchen cabinets, the tacky religious wallpaper in the living room, and a curious brown-and-gold clipper ship motif in the master bath. The kitchen carpet was old-lady-hair blue and there was a folk-artsy mural painted on a bedroom wall of Noah and a bunch of animals. Emphasis there on "folk," not "art."

Structurally, we loved the house. Aesthetically—well, let's just say it was ready to be profiled for *Schmaltzy Decor Monthly*. The house needed a facelift worse than a six-month-old Shar-Pei. Before setting to work, we photographed the home's various catastrophes of taste. Now, four years later, we laugh at those photos, comparing them with our set of "after" photos, amazed at our willingness (or was it naiveté?) to look past the home's appearance and focus instead on its potential. Here's what we learned: a few small cosmetic changes can completely renovate the appearance of a room. Whether you've just bought a house that still exists in the domestic heyday of avocado green and harvest gold, or if you're only looking to breathe a little life into a dull living room, here are a few budget-conscious ways to change the look of your home:

PAINT

The most inexpensive redecorating project is also the one that can yield the most impact: paint. Nothing can update, brighten, or transform a room more effectively than a fresh coat of paint. While many are tempted to paint over dingy walls with a fresh neutral coat of white or cream, I suggest being a little more imaginative. These days, contemporary living spaces are steadily moving toward off-white colors—*way* off-white, like yellows, reds, oranges and deep blues. Don't be afraid to be bold. A daring color choice will go a long way in immediately redefining the space in your home. Give it a burst of sunshine with a warm yellow, or cool things down with a good Monet blue. Tropical colors are even making in-roads in today's homes, from lush greens to bright pinks and feisty oranges.

Before you slap on the paint, take some color samples home from your local home improvement store. Compare them in different types of light (both natural and incandescent) and at various times of the day. Remember that your eye will tend to gravitate toward the darkest or brightest color in the room, which can be an important consideration if you're combining several colors in your redecorating scheme. Don't forget to weigh how colors will look with existing furniture, trim, woodwork—anything that will survive the facelift.

A quick note about paint: While you shouldn't completely disregard paint quality, unless you're planning on keeping the same paint on your walls for the next three presidential administrations, I don't recommend buying expensive paint. If you're like most people I know, your preferences change as often as your calendar pages. Should that be the case, you're no better off with a gallon of thirty-dollar designer paint than a ten-dollar gallon from Sears.

FURNITURE

The paint helped, but what about our hideous couch? Ah … the hideous couch. Our first one was the color of rust, and not in a good *Southern Living* kind of way, but in a fake-wood-paneled-basement kind of way. In those situations, it's easy to repaint your walls and then cleverly use that as an excuse to buy a new couch, one that will match better. You're certainly free to proceed down that road if you prefer. But if it were truly an option, you wouldn't be reading this book, now, would you?

So quit dreaming of Pottery Barn and pay attention. The best way to transform a couch, ottoman, or upholstered chair? Slipcovers. Slipcovers are ideal for updating, and they're easy to clean (just remove and wash). With patterns available at any fabric store, slipcovers are a perfect way to give old chairs a brand-new look. Of course, a prerequisite is the ability to sew—or at least knowing someone with that ability.

Wooden chairs with padded, fabric-covered seats—such as dining room chairs or side chairs—can be easily livened up with a simple fabric replacement. Reupholstering them is a relatively simple procedure, as most seats consist of a piece of wood, cushioning material, and a fabric wraparound. Pick out a nice material (a cotton-polyester blend works best), remove the seat frame and the original fabric, and cut a new cover using the old one as a pattern. Attach the new cover with a staple gun. The hardest part of the process is keeping the fabric taut on all sides as you secure it. It can be a two-person job, but with a little practice, you can bring an old set of chairs back to life.

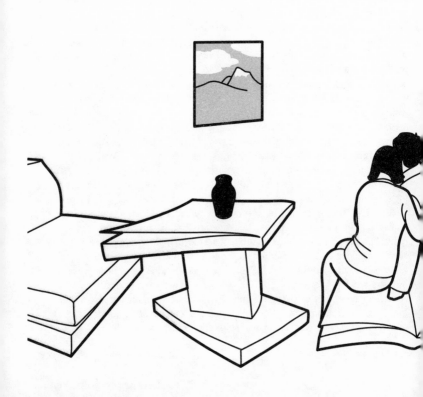

And don't forget about repainting. A fresh application of paint can restore almost any piece of outdated furniture, from wooden chairs to dressers or tables. Clean the surface, paint on a bonding primer (necessary for glossy or polished surfaces), lightly sand, then follow with an oil-based paint. As with painting walls, don't be afraid to experiment with bright, dramatic colors. If you're unsatisfied with the look, just paint it again.

ACCENTS

Call attention to other areas of your home with well-placed design accents:

• Pillows. Cover ugly old pillows with a new, modern fabric. One attractive silk or velvet pillow, or a combination of pillows with different fabrics but a single color theme, can dress up a dull couch. Mix and match. For new pillows, check discount stores like Wal-Mart or Target, each of which has a surprising selection at decent prices.

• Windows. Drape inexpensive, simple fabrics over a rod to jump-start an unattractive window. Remnants or even bed sheets are inexpensive substitutes for "real" window dressing. Try unorthodox hardware like copper piping or other plumbing materials. Or, instead of a rod, drape fabric over angled tiebacks.

• Hardware. A great way to spruce up cabinetry or a dresser is by replacing your old pulls with new ones. Fancier hardware can be expensive, but eBay and merchandise liquidator and/or wholesale stores often have great deals. Or you can make your own. As always, don't immediately discount more whimsical designs—you can always replace and return them if necessary. Regardless, a new set of cabinet and drawer pulls can go a long way in embellishing a room.

It's easy to give your living space a new look by remodeling or refurnishing. But for those of us on shoestring budgets, it's all about the subtle changes— which often can be more satisfying (and, financially speaking, less painful) than the big ones. Make a plan, make a list, and get to work.

Cheap Ways To Create Home Décor

By Margaret Feinberg

Adding your own personal style to your home doesn't have to cost a fortune. A little time and creativity can do wonders for any room. Remember to build upon your existing decor (if you have any) rather than try to remodel everything. Try not to go overboard with trends; they become dated far too quickly. Televisions shows such as *Trading Spaces* are packed with budget ideas and worth a few afternoons or evenings of viewing time.

A TOUCH OF ART

Art comes in all forms, and it's important to keep an open mind. Rather than pay big bucks for original art, look for printed art or even create some of your own. Take a watercolor, oil painting, or sculpting class. Create a collage or a small statue out of papier-mâché.

If you prefer other people's artwork to your own, try buying artwork at garage or moving sales. Shop poster stores when they're having sales. If you know any artists, hint to them about creating a special piece as a gift for an upcoming birthday or holiday such as Christmas.

Keep an eye out for inexpensive artwork. Colorful postcards, greeting cards, pictures from children's books, and images from calendars can be framed for a fraction of the original art's cost. Quilts and fabrics can also be framed for artwork.

Art is printed or painted in off-sizes. Rather than pay for framing, do it yourself. Go through your attic or a Saturday morning's worth of yard sales with a tape measure and try to find a matching frame. You may need to sand or even repaint a frame to make it match your artwork. If you can't find one, visit local retail stores and mass merchants to find good deals on standard frames and matte the work yourself. Stores such as Hobby Lobby and Michael's sell mattes, and if you buy a matte at the store they will often frame the artwork for a reasonable cost. If you plan on matting a lot of artwork, consider buying a matte cutter.

JUST THE RIGHT TOUCH

It's usually the little things that make the biggest difference. Look for ways to add your own creative touch to the details of a room. Use inexpensive accessories such as pillows, plants, vases, plates, or lamps to brighten up a room and create atmosphere. Remember that you can always upgrade an old accessory with a new coat of paint. If you need to buy a rug, remember that two smaller ones are usually less expensive than one larger one.

If you have an unsightly stain or hole in the wall, use a twin or crib quilt to hide the damage. Place a large plant in an unsightly corner or use a plant to hide an air-conditioning unit. Use baskets to store towels in the bathrooms and gift baskets to decorate quiet corners of the room. Don't forget to add potpourri, candles, and other aroma-producing goods throughout your home to add to the ambiance.

CURTAINS

When it comes to curtains, it's time to get creative. If you can't find a set on sale, then visit the linen department of the store. Borrow a sewing machine and use sheets to create curtains or valances. Remember to make the curtains extra long. Short curtains give a room the feeling of bareness.

Use ribbon, textured cords, hair ribbons, or even men's ties to tie the curtains back. You may want to pick up an extra set of sheets. They can be sewn together to create a duvet cover at a third or less of the cost of buying one, and also used to cover an old couch instead of replacing it.

If you have access to a sewing machine, you can save a small fortune. Always visit the reduced price fabric stacks at stores. Create several decorative throws or afghans out of one store-bought comforter or quilt. Drape them over furniture to add color and hide any stains or tears. Consider sewing your own pillows from scratch. If you don't have the time or talent, purchase less expensive pillows and decorate them by adding ribbons, buttons, or other designs.

COLOR ME BEAUTIFUL

Most major paint stores, hardware stores, and home centers such as Lowe's, Sears, and Home Depot sell paint that was mis-mixed for a fraction of original cost. The premium quality paint that someone else didn't want may be perfect for your redesign. Call and ask local stores about their selection and prices.

Consider painting a picture or image on your wall. If you don't have a ton of artistic talent (or even if you do), use an overhead projector to place the image on a wall or canvas. Then trace the outline, rather than painting it freehand. If you're tackling your child's room, visit *www.wallnutz.com* to purchase a reasonably priced paint by number mural kit. Use stencils or an inexpensive wallpaper border to add to a room.

To create borders, use stencils. Use craft paint, which is less expensive than premium paint, to add the details. Consider creating your own stencils by using plastic or cardboard and a knife. (Please be careful!) Use designs from magazines or books to pencil the design you want, and then cut away.

A LEATHERY LOOK

You can use brown paper grocery bags to add texture to individual items such as picture frames, trashcans, or furniture. Begin by tearing the bags into strips and chunks. Mix white glue, such as Elmer's, with water in a bowl until it has a thin consistency. Dip paper in the glue mixture, drain off extra liquid, and layer in random patterns on individual items. It's like papier-mache, but when dried will have a texture and look similar to aged leather.

LIGHTEN UP

You can change the atmosphere of a room by changing the lighting. What kinds of lamps are you using? Could any of them be repainted? How would a different shaped shade or light bulb wattage affect them? Can dimmer switches be added to any of your lighting? Consider buying a new shade rather than replacing an entire lamp. Visit mass merchants such as Target and Wal-Mart for great prices. Make sure you unplug all lamps before painting or rewiring.

GET CREATIVE

Wonderful decor can be found at rummage and garage sales. Look for great prices, but also look for a product's potential. Which items can be given a new coat of paint and a new purpose? Old planters can be painted and rolled in the sand to add texture and a new look. Flower vases can be turned into fish bowls. An old chair can become a plant stand. Jewelry can be used to decorate or accentuate picture frames and lampshades. A mirror can be framed. An old paint roller pan can be painted, decorated and used to hold newspapers and magazines. Old windows can be used as frames for artwork. Add little quotes or pieces of wisdom to your creations to make them truly unique.

CHEAP WAYS TO FURNISH A HOUSE

By Margaret Feinberg

Successful furniture shopping requires a little planning. You'll need a tape measure, notepad, pen, and budget. Draw an outline of the rooms that need furniture and find out the size range of pieces. You may want to consider establishing a furniture fund by selling off pieces you don't want at a garage sale and using the money toward newer furniture.

SECONDHAND OPTIONS

If at all possible, buy furniture secondhand. Garage sales, moving sales, and thrift stores are all great havens for used furniture. Scan the classifieds for furniture sales and call early in the morning after the paper is distributed. Good furniture and good deals go quickly. Remember that you can always reupholster, buy a cover, or repaint to help the piece match your decor. Old shelves can be sanded and refinished. An old chair can be recovered. An end table can be covered with linen to hide damage or stains.

Consider posting want ads at the post office, supermarket, library, church, and workplace about your specific needs. Also pay a visit to local colleges and universities at the end of terms. Students often discard couches, chairs, tables, and other pieces of furniture upon graduation and rather than placing the items in storage. A little dumpster digging can turn up some real treasures.

Talk to local interior decorators. They can tell you of any hotels, condominiums, or large homes that may be renovating and selling furniture at reduced costs. They'll also be able to recommend reasonable furniture stores and outlets.

Ask family members, friends, and neighbors if they have furniture tucked away in an attic or basement. Family and friends may allow you to use furniture at no cost, making it easy if you ever choose to move.

While it can be pricey, some treasures are tucked in the corners of antique shops. Amidst the higher priced items, storekeepers will usually include a few lower fare options. It may be well worth an afternoon of antiquing with a friend. Flea markets can also contain some great finds. Don't be turned off by furniture that is a little worn. Well-built furniture will last longer than newer, lower quality pieces over the long haul.

IF NEW IS FOR YOU

If new is for you, there are a number of options. You may try using a local crafts-man. Most towns have local woodworkers who specialize in custom furniture and can create incredible pieces for below retail. Visit antique stores, furniture repair shops, and even lumberyards for recommendations.

Another option is to buy unfinished furniture and finish it yourself. Besides saving money, this offers a number of advantages. Unfinished manufactures often use a higher grade of lumber because they can't hide defects such as knots or discoloration. Because the furniture is unfinished, you can to select the stain and paint colors to match your decor. You can also cover the furniture with fabric and make a decision at a later date. And there's always the satisfaction of saying you did it yourself.

If you venture into the world of furniture retail, head to mass merchants first. If you have a membership, stores such as Sam's Club and Costco are great places to start. They offer a surprising variety of indoor and outdoor furniture. Don't forget to stop by Target and Wal-Mart for some of your smaller pieces. Before you head to a furniture store, do research. Make a list of what you need and how much you can spend before you walk in, lest you get lured into over purchasing. Remember that most furniture prices are negotiable. Furniture salespeople usually work on commission and will trim the price if sales can go through quickly. Furniture stores usually offer their most publicized sales around holidays. Ask if they have an area of damaged furniture. Study the prices and what it would be take to repair the item.

Look for items with straightforward cuts. A table with straight legs will cost less than a comparable item with curved ones. Remember that if you don't like the metal knobs on a piece of furniture you can upgrade later. It's a good idea to invest in stain-resistant upholstery and avoid light-colored or easily stain-able colors.

And remember that you don't always have to go big. Smaller pieces can do wonders to fill and liven up a room. Decorator tables, those inexpensive circles of wood, can be dressed up with a tablecloth or linen. Place a lamp, candle, and framed photograph on top to create a warm display in the corner of a room.

Always comparison-shop before you buy. Even if the salesman is offering you what he calls "an incredible deal," check it out with other stores before buying and use your knowledge to negotiate a lower price or at least extra services such as home delivery and fabric cleaning.

Bring a camera along with you and take photos of the piece you purchase. That way you have proof if anything is inaccurately shipped. Buy floor room models when available. Whether it's from the showroom floor or local model homes, these items can be picked up at a discount.

Visit legitimate furniture factory outlets. Top name furniture is often discounted because it has been overstocked, discontinued, or displayed at trade shows. Some outlets will actually help cover travel costs based on a minimum order. Shop in person whenever possible, and calculate freight costs before making a final purchase. If travel isn't practical, consider ordering over the phone, but remember that you're taking a bigger risk on what you actually get. You can also build your own furniture. While some pieces, including dressers and chairs, may be challenging, tables and shelves can be put together without too much difficulty. Back issues of *Amateur Woodworker* are extremely helpful.

CHEAP WAYS TO BUY
AND MAINTAIN YOUR CAR By Margaret Feinberg

Like a house, a car can either be a blessing or become a money pit. Here are some ways to steer clear from spending too much on your vehicle.

KNOW HOW TO BUY NEW

Before you begin shopping for a new or used vehicle, you need to have an idea of what you want. Which features are important to you? Which features can you live without? How much can you afford to spend? Are you attracted to any particular models, colors, or styles? Before stepping on a car lot, talk to your friends and neighbors. What cars do they drive? What are their strengths and weaknesses? Have they ever owned a car they wouldn't want to own again? If someone is particularly proud of his car, kindly ask if you can drive it a few blocks.

It's no secret that new cars lose between 10 and 20 percent when you drive them off the lot, but if you're set on buying a new car, here are a few tips. Every car on the dealership lot has a MSRP, a manufacturer's standard retail price. This is known as the sticker price. You should always ask to see the manufacturer's invoice on a new vehicle. This is the price the manufacturer actually paid. Make sure the invoice matches the serial number and offer $250 to $500 over invoice. Ask if there's any dealer or customer cash provided from the manufacturer.

Always buy a vehicle at the end of the month, and if possible buy in December. At the end of the year, dealerships get paid a percentage based on the amount of cars they sell that year. If they sell a certain number of a particular vehicle, they get bonus money, so naturally dealerships want to get their numbers up before January 1. Avoid buying new edition or special edition vehicles. Generally they are in such high demand that dealerships are unwilling to make deals on them.

If you can't wait until December to buy a new car, begin shopping in August. New models are released between June and September, which puts dealerships under pressure to move out the old and make room for the new.

Ask how many days the car has been on the lot. The longer the car is in the dealer's possession, the more insurance expenses they incur. Ideally, dealerships want to turn over their stock every thirty days. Some cars will remain on a lot for six months. They don't sell because they're overpriced or people don't want them for various reasons. Occasionally, dealerships will sell vehicles at a loss.

Buy four-wheel drive vehicles in the summer, and sports cars in the winter. You'll get a better deal. The inverse is also true. Trade in sports cars in the spring,

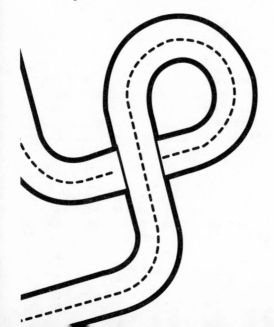

and trucks in the fall because that is when the majority of people buy them.

Always test-drive a variety of vehicles to prevent buyers' remorse. Few, if any, companies will take a car back once purchased.

Also, talk to your insurance agent before you buy. A four-door car is considered safer than a two-door car. A four-cylinder car will be less to insure than a six-cylinder car.

USED TO YOUR ADVANTAGE

As you begin looking at used cars, you need to be able know their actual value. NADA (National Auto Dealers Association) can be purchased at a gas station or on the Internet and can provide the value of vehicles made in the last ten years. It will tell you wholesale a retail value according to the miles. It will give you an idea. Kelly Blue Book, *www.kbb.com*, is another starting point to find out what a vehicle is worth. When it comes to the actual value of a car, the bottom line is that it's still what you can actually buy and sell it for.

There are a number of alternatives to buying cars from the classified ads. While buying a car from a friend may provide savings, keep in mind that it can strain the relationship if something goes wrong with the vehicle. Rental companies often turn over their fleets every few years. Some rental companies are willing to sell directly to the consumer, while others will turn them over to a dealership who will usually certify them before reselling the vehicles. Call local rental companies and ask if they have any vehicles for sale.

Automobile auctions take place on a regular basis around the country, but usually these sales are limited to dealership personnel and those in the auto industry. If you know someone who can buy one for you, attend an auction with him.

Always take the car to a mechanic to have it looked over, even if you're buying from a dealership that certifies the car.

Try to buy a car with a manufacturer's warranty. If you're buying a car from an individual, the extended warranty is usually passed along. If you're buying a car from a dealership, the extended warranty may not carry through. Know your warranty, its limitations, and if it can be transferred to you.

You can find general reviews and recommendations of cars at *www.lemonaidcars.com*. If a car is considered a lemon, under law the manufacturer or dealer may be called to replace parts or repurchase it. You can visit the website *www.carfax.com* and enter the serial number of the car you want to buy to find out if it has been in a major accident.

FINANCING

Financing is where most dealerships make money. There are some great financing opportunities with low interest rates on new cars. In order to qualify you're going to need a good credit rating. You can find out your credit rating by visiting *www.freecreditreport.com* or *www.icreditreports.com*. Generally, the more money you have as a down payment, the better the interest rate you'll receive. Beware of being sold too much vehicle for what you can afford.

MAINTENANCE

Consider talking to a mechanic about a car before you buy it. Ask about common problems or weaknesses related to the vehicle's machinery or design.

As far as maintenance, you probably already know the basics. Change your oil every three thousand miles or so. Keep good tires on your vehicle to protect your alignment. Study and follow your manufacturer's suggested maintenance program.

Keep your car clean. This is especially true if you plan to trade your car in. Invest in a set of seat covers to protect and maintain the car's value. If you smoke in your car, it will lessen the value. Dog and cat hair can be hard to remove from upholstery. The dealership will take you more seriously if you drive in with a clean car. Also, dress up. Show the dealership that you actually care about your vehicle and personal appearance.

While trading services with a friend—computer consultation for auto repair—can save you a significant amount of money, take it to the dealership if it's still under warranty. Consider taking an auto course from a local college or school to learn the basics and to hopefully learn to do some things on your own.

CHEAP WAYS TO DECORATE A WALL

By Jason Boyett

Walls are like Christmas trees. They come in all shapes and sizes, and no two people decorate them alike. Some throw just about anything on their Christmas tree, from Aunt Rose's crocheted manger scene to the abstract crayon mess little Jimmy brought home from preschool. Others are highly organized, richly adorned with matching cream and burgundy velvet ribbons, and nothing else (after all, the themed tree has no room for tacky). Then you have the venerable tree from Charlie Brown's Christmas special, the stunning transformation of which comes about due only to a string or two of well-placed tinsel and some tricky animation. It's a Christmas miracle!

Well, maybe that's too dramatic. Try this: It's a convoluted pop-cultural metaphor! That's better.

Like Charlie Brown's listless shrub, a lifeless, mundane wall can become a striking visual anchor of your home with a few thoughtful decorations. And by decorations, I don't mean Harley posters or neon beer signs or cutesy bulletin board collages of all your sorority friends. I'm talking about classier decor, like stuffed elk heads.

Just kidding, of course—taxidermy can be really expensive. Instead, let's look at some tight-fisted ways to add visual punch to an ordinary wall.

PAINT

You'll find a more detailed discussion of this in "Cheap Ways to Give a Room a Facelift," but it's worth mentioning again: Nothing redefines a room more dramatically and cost-efficiently than a new coat of paint. My advice is to be bold. Experiment with color. Try a cornflower blue, a sunny yellow, or a calming shade of green. Keeping with the tortuous metaphor, paint is the star on top of the Christmas tree.

FRAMED PHOTOGRAPHY

I once recommended to a friend that he have a set of family photographs developed into black-and-white prints, rather than color. He looked at me as if I'd just asked him to churn his own butter, his agitated stare suggesting that black-and-white photography was the unsophisticated and immature cousin of modern Kodachrome. Philistine. What he didn't realize was this: in a color-rich world, black-and-white photographs convey a greater sense of detail, depth and poignancy than your average color photo. Plus, they look really, really cool.

Film processing has come a long way in the last few years, and now most processing centers can make black-and-white prints from color film. To add a striking bit of artistry to your wall, select some favorite snapshots—nature, portraits, moments of spontaneity—and have black-and-white prints made from the original negatives. Then, visit your nearest craft store, discount store or frame shop. Purchase a bunch of ready-made black frames with wide, pre-cut white mattes. For three- by five-inch photos, an eleven- by fourteen-inch matted frame is ideal. The expansive matte board helps define the photo, and the crisp effect can be striking—particularly when several matching frames are grouped on a brightly colored wall.

I did exactly this with some family photos taken from a little point-and-shoot Olympus. My wife bought the frames on clearance at a craft store for something like three dollars a pop. A photographer friend of mine—one whose tastes are very refined—asked me who custom-framed my photography. I didn't tell him it was me. Nor did I tell him that the entire grouping cost less than one of his custom frames. Even better, he couldn't tell the difference.

FRAMED ART

Take the same approach as the suggestion above, but this time use inexpensive prints made from the work of your favorite artists. Where exactly will you get these nicely printed, ready-to-frame works of art? Not from the art prints section of the frame shop, or at the store in the mall. Nope. You'll get them from calendars.

Trust me—no one will know, particularly if you house the artwork in a classy frame-and-white-matte arrangement. Most wall calendars today come printed on high-quality stock, and the only difference between their three hundred dollar Thomas Kinkaid print and your six dollar calendar one will be a smaller size and the lack of a signature. But what's a signature, really, other than a massive profit center for the Painter of Light ™?

For beautiful monochrome nature photography, purchase an Ansel Adams calendar. Get funkier with Picasso, or colorful and edgy with the work of the late Keith Haring. If you choose, stick with the classic brush strokes of Monet or Van Gogh. For those with more distinct tastes, there are calendars of African

masks, Japanese scrolls and screens, even photos of exotic textiles and fabrics. Don't go to the expense of store-bought prints. By removing the art from a calendar, you can create a wall that truly impresses. People will think you've pilfered a museum.

FRAMES WITHOUT PHOTOGRAPHY OR ART

Why include artwork when the frame is so interesting? Don't laugh—more and more interior designers are going artless with old, picture-free frames. You can find empty frames at any thrift shop, yard sale or estate auction. Buy as many as you want, paying special attention to those with unique carvings and designs.

The trick is to transform the frames once you get home. Often, all they need is a good cleaning. Some designers recommend painting them with a soft-hued wash—don't cover the frame completely, but use a rough, dry-brush stroke to accent the woodwork. Make a casual grouping on the wall, or display the frames on a shelf. Think of it as art for the artless.

SHELVES

A set of two or three matching shelves is a great way to add class to a wall while allowing you to keep a revolving décor. Many craft stores offer unfinished, unpainted pine shelving at great prices. For a crisp, modern look, paint your shelves bright white. Or you may prefer a wood stain with a protective coat of polyurethane (Ideally, you just want your shelves to match the room's trim and molding, if you have it).

Mount the shelves to the wall in a staggered grouping, then show off your favorite collectibles or other displays (dried flowers, candles, Pez dispensers—it's all good). Propping a framed photograph or artwork against the wall (placing non-slip tabs at the base of the frame) allows you to easily substitute other pictures to keep the look fresh. Change the contents of the shelves seasonally, or whenever you get bored with them.

WALL HANGINGS

Decorative throw rugs, heirloom quilts, and other attractive fabrics can also add interest to a wall. Again, to avoid getting fleeced on expensive commercially manufactured "heirlooms," first explore your community's yard sales, thrift stores, and even Grandma's attic. Make sure you get Grandma's permission first, because some seniors can be downright nasty about their quilts.

The least expensive way to display a wall hanging is by first hemming the top of the material to create a loop—this is what the curtain rod goes through. Stores like Target or Wal-Mart carry attractive, inexpensive rods and finials (the pointy little doo-dads at the end of the rod). Next step: Hang it on the wall. A good idea is to group your hanging below a shelf of the same approximate width. In fact, many shelves are available in a single-unit rod/shelf combo.

Walls, like empty Christmas trees, can be daunting. (Who's tired of this metaphor? Okay, okay, me too. Put your hands down.) Walls, like a painter's blank canvas, can be daunting. To make one come alive, though, you only need the swift twin brush strokes of creativity and artistic arrangement. You'll also need a couple bucks. And calendars. And maybe a camera. And some paint, if you decide it's worth it. But that's all. Really.

CHEAP WAYS TO BUY A COMPUTER

By Jason Boyett

Before you begin the process of buying a computer, you need to ask yourself whether you really need one. If you want to play games, then buy a PlayStation2. If you want to take pictures using a digital camera, consider buying a printer that accepts memory cards from a digital camera and prints without a computer. If you want to use instant messenger, then pick up the telephone. The computer industry and the media would like everyone to believe that they have to have a PC, but the primary use of a computer is as a business tool. If you are looking for ways to cut back, an investment in a computer may not be the answer.

If, however, you know why you're buying a computer and what you intend to use it for, there are a lot of options and cheaper is not always better. Would you buy a car whose maximum speed was thirty-five miles per hour just because it was cheaper? It's worth it to pay for a computer that meets your needs and can be upgraded as technology develops.

Computers are upgraded so quickly and have become so reasonably priced that it's hard to justify saving a little money by buying used. In addition, the real expense of computers is setting up and configuring the software that you will be using. When you buy new, the operating system and software drivers are installed and tested. The value of this is priceless. Another challenge in buying used is insuring that all the software you need is installed and available. You'll want to make sure the computer comes with a recovery disk to recover the system to its original state. Without this you will have to suffer through all the junk the previous owner might have installed. That software could be a plus, but it could also slow things down, and uninstalling is not always the best way to go.

Buying new is highly encouraged. The best prices are usually clone PC (i.e. non-name brand). Mom-and-pop-managed computer stores usually sell new and used PCs and have experts that can answer any of your questions (as opposed to any salesman at chain office supply or electronic stores). If you ever have any difficulties, you can drop your computer off and let them deal with the problem. These stores are usually family run and you can feel good about supporting a small business in your community.

Like mom and pop specialty stores, major chain electronic and office supply stores allow you to buy a computer instantly and avoid any shipping charges. Unfortunately, many of these stores have less-than-knowledgeable sales staff who are encouraged to push the extras such as extended warranties and added features because of their commission-based pay. If you don't know much about computers you can quickly have the wool pulled over your eyes, as features such as a fast processor are emphasized while a small memory is overlooked. Computer-only retail stores offer a wider variety and a generally a more knowledgeable staff, and are more likely to accommodate returns and exchanges. They tend to keep close tabs on their competitors and offer good prices.

Mail order is another alternative. Magazines such as *Computer Shopper* allow you to order the exact machine you desire. You usually don't need to pay shipping, but will be required to pay freight. Always choose the lowest freight costs available, since this is an area where companies try to pad their pockets. And always pay with a credit card rather than mail order to provide protection against faulty companies or products.

Computer shows and fairs offer another alternative for buying computers. The same factors need to be weighed when deciding upon a purchase. You may find good prices from large corporations who are upgrading their computers and laptops, too. Remember when buying a used computer to look at the memory capabilities and consider investing a little extra for more. It will allow your computer to run smoother and better.

You can also cut out the middleman by purchasing a computer directly from the company. Or consider buying a refurbished computer directly from it.

Another option is to buy via eBay. A good laptop can be priced from $1,500 to $2,000 and via eBay you can save five hundred dollars or more. Some of these laptops are even new, and are sold by liquidators as "used" because a new model has been released. The risk is that you are buying a PC without an operating system or other software. You will have to read the detailed descriptions.

If anyone throws in an added feature or bonus, you can check out its true value at *www.pricewatch.com* and find out what it's truly worth.

Your final decision needs to be weighed by a number of factors. What do you need from your computer? What features are you getting for your money? What additional features, if any, does that price include, such as warranties, telephone technical support, or on-site servicing?

CALL IN THE TROOPS

If you are new to computers or consider yourself technically challenged, then you need to find someone you know who is willing to help you throughout the process. This may be a friend, family member, in-law, neighbor, or anyone else you can round up to donate some of his time.

Most teenagers know more about setting up computers than their teachers do. Talk to a teenager or a hungry college student and have them over for dinner. It's a great investment that can save you time and money. You might even make a new friend in the process.

SAVE ON MONITORS

One of the biggest areas you can save money in is when buying a monitor. Used monitors are often 35 to 75 percent less than a new one. You may even know a friend or family member who will give you one. Monitors tend to last a long time, and if you're looking to save money, a used monitor is a great place to start unless you're using the computer for anything design related. If you're involved in desktop publishing or web design, you should invest in a top quality monitor. Or if you have eye problems, however, it may be worth investing in a larger, newer screen.

HOOKING UP

Retail merchants often offer rebates or discounts for signing up with a particular server for several years. It can be a faux-savings, especially when you consider Juno (*www.juno.com*), which offers free email service and limited Internet access. A year's worth of twenty to twenty-five dollar a month fees adds up to two to three hundred dollars a year. On the other hand, if you prefer a name brand Internet provider, it can be a nice added bonus.

GOING TO PRINT

Buyers of ink jet printers know the cost isn't in the printer, it's in the ink. Most inexpensive ink jet printers are equivalent in function and provide all the necessary functions for home use. Older ink jet printers are practically given away, but before picking up a used printer, make sure it comes with everything needed for installation. Generic ink cartridges are often available for older ink jet printers, so this can save you over the long run. But generally, it's safer to go ahead and invest in a new ink jet printer. If you plan on printing a lot, then compare the prices of ink before buying the printer.

If you're looking for quality printing, you may want to upgrade to the laser jet printer. While they are more expensive, the speed and quality of laser printers are much higher, and the ink lasts much longer. Some people find it cost effective to print in black and white on their laser jet and color on the ink jet printers.

KEEPING YOUR FRIENDS

Much like a car, it's usually not a good idea to buy a used computer from a friend. Unless the friend is a computer geek demanding the latest and greatest, the machines will have lost the majority of their value and could cause big headaches and strain your relationship in the long run.

CHEAP WAYS TO MAKE
OUR OWN HOUSEHOLD PRODUCTS

By Margaret Feinberg

If only it was just spring that we had to clean. The day-in, day-out process of keeping things clean can be a grimy affair. Fortunately, you can escape having to buy name brand products with a little time and research.

INTRO TO MIXTURES

Bleach can whiten almost anything and makes a great disinfectant and mildew killer. It should generally be diluted before using. Ammonia is great for cleaning glass surfaces and cutting grease. It can also strip wax. Cornstarch and baking soda can be used to remove odors and stains. White vinegar can be used to disinfect, remove stains and odors, cut grease, and clean hard surfaces. Specific cleaning recipes can be found at *www.practicalkitchen.com*.

It's important to look at labels of products before mixing any or experimenting with any new concoctions. Never, ever mix ammonia, bleach and/or vinegar; it could result in a toxic gas. Avoid mixing cousin products—which may contain traces of ammonia, vinegar, or bleach—together.

Buy your products in bulk and keep stored in airtight containers. You may want to consider storing ammonia and bleach in completely different rooms for safety, and always keep these products out of the reach of children.

GENERAL STAIN REMOVERS

Hydrogen peroxide is great for removing bloodstains. It can also be used to shine up faucets in your sinks and bath area. Soda water, if applied immediately, can help lift stains out of fabrics.

To remove rust stains, combine cream of tartar and hydrogen peroxide into a paste. Apply and wash out.

Shaving cream can be used to remove stains from carpeting. Simply spray on, let sit, and wipe with a dry rag. Always test a spot before tackling a larger area. Liquid dishwasher detergent can be used to remove residue in bathtubs and shower. Rub on sides, let dry, and rinse. Ice can be used to remove gum. Simply hold an ice cube against the gum until it hardens and remove. Or place the entire article in the freezer. Products such as Goo Gone and De-Solv-It are great for removing adhesive and stickers.

WINDOW WASHERS

There are a variety of mixes you can create to clean windows. Some testify to adding cornstarch to water, while others prefer vinegar. Always use lint-free materials when wiping the surface. Paper towels can be effective but expensive. Instead, use an old shirt, newspapers, or a clean chalkboard eraser to remove streaks.

Instead of buying name brand window cleaners, consider buying car window cleaner. It's generally sold in a larger size for less money and does the same job. Save your old spray bottles and refill.

VINEGAR

Combine a touch of vinegar with water to clean hardwood floors. You can run a few tablespoons of white vinegar combined with a full pot of water through your coffee maker to remove abrasive stains. Flush through with several pots of water afterward.

You can create your own baby wipes by buying sturdy paper towels, placing them in a large Ziploc with baby oil and baby powder, and diluting them with water.

BLEACH

While you should always be careful when working with bleach so you don't discolor clothes or other materials, bleach can be used as an excellent disinfectant. Combine bleach and water in a ten-to-one ratio and use to disinfect bathrooms and kitchens.

LEMONY FRESH

To help alleviate unpleasant odors in garbage disposals, cut up a lemon and grind it up in the disposal. Allow hot water to run through the system afterward. This will help unpleasant-smelling food pass through the system and will leave you with a lemony fresh scent.

PRESERVING RAZORS AND SHOWER CURTAINS

There's a reason why most razors are disposable. The blades become dull and rust slowly grows along the edges. In order to add life to your razors, always dry them after using and, if possible, add a thin layer of Vaseline after use to preserve and protect the blade.

Another option is to store them in the freezer, where they won't rust as quickly. This also works for steel wool pads used to scrub stubborn pot and pan stains. Instead of throwing away grimy shower curtains, place them in the washing machine with your regular detergent. Send them through one, and if needed, two gentle cycles. They should come through looking new.

CLEANING SUPPLIES

Use old clothes for rags to dust, clean, and scrub. Socks can be worn on the hands as dust mitts. Use an old shirt to remove streaks from mirrors and glass after cleaning.

You can create your own glass cleaner by combining one cup of ammonia and a tablespoon of liquid dish detergent in a spray container. Fill with water. Use to clean bathroom countertops, stoves, windows, and even tile floors. Vinegar and water can also be combined to clean windows.

Use old toothbrushes and nail scrubbers for cleaning small items or hard-to-get-to areas.

MOPPING IT UP

Take old dishtowels and rags and bleach them. Clamp them together with a plastic or metal clamp, attach to a long stick or pole, and you've created your own mop.

You can keep your sponges clean by regularly placing them in the dishwasher for a cycle. To kill bacteria, place a damp sponge in the microwave for twenty to thirty seconds. To avoid odors, always wring sponges clean after use. To remove persistent odors, dip in a bleach-water mixture for a few minutes. Sprinkle with lemon juice.

CHEAP WAYS TO REVITALIZE YOUR COFFEE TABLE By Jason Boyett

The coffee table is dying. In today's fast-paced world, comfort has become the number-one priority of homeowners. The result has been the gradual replacement of the proud coffee table by the upstart ottoman, more and more of which are beginning to take on the multi-tasking characteristics—hidden storage, quirky design—long owned by our mug-supporting friends. Remember the first coffee table you ever had, the thirty-year-old chunk of polyurethaned oak veneer from your grandparents' attic that you hauled off to college? The one with all the Kool-Aid stains? Ah … nostalgia.

It hasn't always been this way. The coffee table came into its own in the late seventies in conjunction with that three-hundred-pound gorilla of publishing, the coffee table book. Large-format, photo-rich tomes on everything from cats to Katmandu, these books were a popular way to appear intelligent, well read, and sophisticated, and they justified the existence of coffee tables even for non-coffee drinkers. Another boost came after the television show "Friends" premiered in 1994, bringing Central Perk and its well-utilized table into the homes of millions of Americans.

But now those glory days seem to be over, as veteran tables are being retired on a weekly basis during episodes of *Trading Spaces*. I, for one, hope the coffee table strikes back at the ottoman empire, and becomes cool again. While the right coffee table book can certainly up the coolness factor a notch or two (A *History of Britain Volume 2: 1603-1776* carries a certain cachet), they usually cost upwards of forty dollars. Your coffee table renaissance can begin less expensively. Here's how:

THE TABLE ITSELF

Some coffee tables are noteworthy to begin with. Antique blanket trunks make great coffee tables, as do old wooden shipping crates. Problem is, those can cost lots of money, particularly if they've been restored. What you're probably wondering is how to make your grandmotherly table interesting again. Here's how: Give it a complete makeover by painting it, and painting it boldly. There is nothing remarkable about a coffee table with the same dark mahogany-stained wood as everyone else. What is interesting is that same coffee table painted orange. Or lime green. Or lilac. Or a rich, golden yellow. Sand it down, clean it up, and color that baby with a nice oil enamel. If you don't like it, you can always buy another half-gallon of paint. You'll be surprised how a piece of sensible furniture can become a room's focal point with a few daring swipes of a paint brush.

THE SURFACE

If it gives you the willies to even think about painting over nice, finished wood, then try something else—decoupage. For the unenlightened (which is to say, males), decoupage is just a fancy word for "cut and paste." Here's how you do it: photocopy pages from old books, family photographs, children's drawings, sheet music, newspaper stories, fabric—anything you want—and artfully arrange them on the surface of your coffee table. Most craft stores carry a special glue called decoupage medium, which you'll use to seal the paper to the surface after you're satisfied with the arrangement (make sure you like the layout before you start gluing). Once you've finished, seal over the paper with extra medium or polyurethane. Finally, measure the dimensions of your surface and have a protective pane of glass cut to rest upon it.

THE STUFF ON THE TABLE

The best way, of course, to invigorate your tired coffee table is to put it to use by covering it with cool stuff. If your table is home only to last month's TV *Guide* and the remote control, then you have seriously underestimated its capacity for entertaining. Coffee tables aren't just for coffee—they're for showing off your personality.

My wife and I have a friend who's deeply into scrapbooking. Every photo she takes will have an eventual home (and caption), but sometimes it takes a while to get filed. She keeps these loose, pre-filed photos in a flat basket in the middle of her coffee table. Inevitably, visitors to her couch reach for the basket. Half an hour later, they've willingly familiarized themselves with her trip to the Caribbean last summer, and the photos trigger another hour or two of stimulating conversation—just because they're within reach.

Coffee tables are also good for displaying an array of magazines. But as you well know, magazine subscriptions and individual newsstand prices can cost money. If you're just looking for a few decorative items that might, ahem, make you appear thoughtful and cultured for your next date, there's a way to get them: Trial subscriptions. Most publications will offer some sort of free trial subscription (details can usually be found on those annoying tear-out cards). The instructions follow along these lines: *Please send me THREE FREE issues of* Coffee Table Digest. *When I receive an invoice, and if I decide to subscribe, I will pay the seventy-five dollar subscription price. If I choose not to subscribe, I'll just write 'CANCEL' on the invoice, send it back and owe nothing.*

Kids, this really does work. I can't tell you how many one- or two-time copies of good magazines, literary journals, and special-interest newsletters I've received using this method. You send in the card, you get the product, and you cancel the bill. Sometimes, due to customer-service snafus, your bill gets withdrawn but the subscription never does. I've been receiving a popular Internet publication for two years using this method, and haven't paid a cent. Maybe that's stealing, but I prefer to think of it as taking advantage of a flawed marketing gimmick. One thing I know: A coffee table with the latest issues of *The Oxford American*, *The Skeptical Enquirer*, *Fast Company*, *Kitchen and Bath Design News*, and *Spelunker Flophouse* is undoubtedly an attention-grabbing piece of furniture.

THE COFFEE PART

Don't call it a coffee table unless you're going to actually use it to support coffee mugs. It's only a matter of integrity (sorely needed after acquiring all those free magazines). Why not use your coffee table to display your most eclectic coffee mugs and coasters? One guy I know habitually takes home one of those promotional cardboard coasters that are regularly stacked on restaurant tables. He has his dining companions sign and date the coaster, then adds it to his huge collection in a coffee table drawer as a memento of his evening. Others collect coffee mugs—I make a practice of buying a mug from every fly-fishing shop I enter on my quest to find the perfect Rocky Mountain trout stream. Random collectibles are always interesting.

Coffee tables intrinsically have more character than an ottoman and offer you, as the owner of a piece of fine furniture, countless ways to express your individuality through them. Fire up the coffee pot and put your table to work.

CHEAP WAYS TO FIND A PET

By Josh Hatcher

Pets keep us company. They make us happy. They give us all the enjoyment of a relationship without all that meaningless emotional and conversational garbage getting in the way. There are countless books and articles written to help you determine which pet is right for you. They are full of lists of rare and expensive breed animals that require special diets and diamond studded collars in order to survive. For most of us, the right pet is the one with the right price. After all, it's just an animal right? Try these tips to find the right-priced pet for you.

ASK YOURSELF

"Am I ready for this?" Are you sure you know what you are getting into? Most dogs and cats have a life expectancy of at least ten years, some longer. A fish tank is a lot of work. Raising a snake often means you will have to buy feeder mice, and if you are a bit squeamish, forget it. Yes, it is just an animal, but it means a change in your lifestyle. Be sure that you know all the ramifications of the decision you make. Understand that if you get a pit bull, it may eat you. If you get a lizard, it may stink. If you get a goldfish, it may die. If you get a dog, it may live to be eighteen years old. It's hard to say goodbye to a friend that you have had for that long. Are you ready for the responsibility of cleaning, feeding, and maintaining a pet?

PEDIGREES ARE FOR THE BIRDS

Unless you have the patience, willingness, and love for a particular breed of animal, a pedigreed pet will only put your pocket in a pinch. People spend hundreds to thousands of dollars for a pet based on its bloodline and characteristics. Often, pedigreed pets are weaker, and less healthy because of efforts to keep the bloodlines pure. Pedigrees are investments that take a lot of time and effort to get a return on. Stick with the Great Dane pups next door whose mother met an ambitious Chihuahua. Mutts are usually friendlier, healthier, and definitely cheaper.

PUPPIES AND KITTENS ARE OVERRATED

Everybody thinks the babies are so cute, and who wouldn't want a ball of fluff that squeaks for a pet? But if you wait a few months, the cute little thing will get bigger, and the seller will be more anxious to get rid of it, and probably lower the cost. You miss out on the joy of owning a fur ball, but you miss out on the hassle of having a teething, urinating beast underfoot as well. Often a full-grown pet is a better investment, as house-training has probably already been done. You can save money on carpet cleaning.

SKIP THE PET STORES

Don't waste your money paying for the local pet store's rent, electric bill, and yellow page ad. There are breeders and pet lovers all over who you can buy from directly. If you have to get a pedigreed pet, or a rare thorn headed dung beetle, try to buy from an individual as opposed to a pet store. It could save you considerably.

CLASSIFIEDS, BULLETIN BOARDS, WEBSITES

People are always getting rid of pets. They don't have the time to care for them, are moving to the city, or just decided they don't like tarantulas anymore. Read the paper or look at the bulletin boards at the grocery store, and you'll find hundreds of free or cheap pets. Go online to *www.petfinder.org*. Thousands of dogs, cats, birds, lizards, and man-eating piranhas are being given away or let go for a small donation. Most have already had their shots and been spayed or neutered, thus saving you even more money.

THE SHELTER

Animal shelters and rescue centers are a great place to go. Once again, the animals are already fixed, vaccinated, and groomed for a small donation. There are many breed-specific rescue centers where you can find a rare Chinese Water Dragon or whatever your favorite pet is. There's just something great about taking an animal from a place that wants you to help them. It makes you feel like a pet superhero.

SPRAY OR NEUTER

If you have a mutt, there is no sense in creating a new breed. Your best option is to have your cat or dog fixed. It saves on a lot of aggravation, and mellows your animal's temperament. Spay/USA keeps a list of veterinarians that give discounts on fixing your pet. You can reach them at (800)-248-SPAY. Friends of Animals is another organization that keeps such a list. You can reach them at (800)-321-PET.

BREEDING

If you do have a pedigreed pet, consider the option of breeding. As mentioned earlier, it's not for everyone, and it is a difficult investment, but if you love the breed, and have the dedication, you may be able to get a terrific return on that investment. One litter of pups or kittens, or one clutch of lizard eggs, could increase your initial investment several times over.

SUPPLIES

Twenty-five pounds of dog food is cheaper than five five-pound bags. Cat litter, fish food, and hamster bedding can all be purchased in bigger packages for a cheaper amount per unit. You may have to shell out more cash at once, but it will be a longer amount of time before you have to restock. Pet suppliers often publish coupons, and these can save you a buck or two here and there. Many pets are finicky about their food, but if your pet allows you to try an off brand instead of name brand, you can save even more.

CHEAP WAYS TO GROCERY SHOP

By Josh Hatcher

With a family of five, we often hear, "Your grocery bill must be tremendous!" We could play it up and try to guilt-trip people into donating to the "Save the Hatchers" fund, but honestly, we have found dozens of angles to trim costs, and then we can route the extra grocery money to other parts of the budget.

AUDIT

Before you make a grocery list and go grocery shopping, go through your fridge, your freezer, and your cupboards. You may not have enough to make a meal, but you don't want to go to the store and buy ketchup if you already have three half-empty bottles in your fridge. You won't want to get a whole case of green beans if you already have a several cans on the shelf.

MAKE A LIST

We're strapped for time; we enjoy the convenience of stopping at the Quick-Mart and buying a loaf of bread and a gallon of milk while we pump our gas, even if we have to pay twice as much. But if you take the extra fifteen minutes, plan out your meals, and get only what you need to make them and a few goodies, it'll knock the cost of the impulse spending way down. If you know what you are looking for when you walk in the door, you will spend less than if you decide what you want to eat based on the packaging and in-store advertising. If you need help figuring out how to make a meal plan or a list, check out *BettyCrocker.com*; you can choose your meals and print out the menus and your grocery list in just a few clicks.

SHOP FOR A MONTH

We have saved countless trips to the store and pinched a bunch of pennies by making our meal plan for a month and getting our shopping done all at once. Each time you go to the store, you see something else that you didn't know you wanted before you walked in. The more trips you make, the more stuff you buy, the more money you spend.

Bread freezes, and so do most other things if you take the time to figure out how. If you have a large freezer or a big cupboard for canned and boxed goods, it works great. If you share a cramped apartment with seven cats, you may have to find another idea.

FROM SCRATCH

Make as many meals from scratch as you can. Convenience foods are expensive in comparison to a home-cooked meal. Getting a few of them for those nights when you don't feel like cooking is fine. But for a third of the cost of a TV dinner, you probably could have made the real thing.

SALE PAPERS

They show up in the Sunday paper, they get mailed to "Current Resident," and they usually end up in the trash can. But when you plan out your menu before shopping, try to center it around the items on sale. If turkey breast is on sale for ninety-eight cents per pound, then turkey stew, turkey sandwiches, turkey and rice soup, and turkey salad should all get slapped on the menu. Be sure to clip any coupons, and keep in mind that some stores will double coupon value.

DON'T SHOP HUNGRY

Want to see your grocery bill shrink? Eat before you shop. There is a reason manufactures spend so much money making the packaging look attractive. It appeals to your stomach. The size of the emptiness in your stomach is directly proportional to the length of the receipt at the end of your shopping trip.

STORE BRANDS

Everyone has gone to a friend's house when they were kids and seen the boxes of "Lucky Shapes" and "Toasted Oat Krunchies" instead of Lucky Charms and Cheerios. But to tell you the truth, most store brand items are manufactured by the same company, in the same factory, even on the same machine. Store brands are often 20 to 30 percent less than the big names. So don't let them poke fun at your fake Dr. Pepper or your generic Hamburger Helper.

BUY BULK OF YOUR FAVORITES

If you are a lover of green beans or a peanut butter freak, check with the store manager to see if they can cut you a deal on a case of peanut butter. You may be able to knock off half the price of each item in the case! But if you eat microwaveable macaroni only once a month, don't buy six cases. For the things you use the least, you should buy only what you know you will use.

BARGAIN STORES

Aldi's, Save-a-lot, and Super Wal-Marts are invading the country, and there is probably a store near you. Even the brand name items are 10 to 20 percent cheaper. Because they buy gig-a-tons of food at a time to fill stores nationwide, they save money and pass some of those savings on to you. Local branches of national bakeries like Stroehman's and WonderBread often have a "Bread Thrift Store" where bread is one day past the "Sell By" date at reduced prices. Twelvegrain bread, which is normally over two bucks, often sells for three loaves a buck. You can't beat it.

NON-FOOD

Do not buy the nonfood items at the grocery store. Paper goods, garbage bags, cleaning supplies, etc. can all be purchased at discount stores or on sale at Wal-Mart or Kmart. Grocery stores only sell them thinking the convenience of buying them at the same time you buy your food will make you not mind spending twice as much.

SPICES

Per pound, spices are probably the most expensive items on your shopping list. Instead of paying three dollars for a bottle, try buying them in bulk from the health food store, or get them three-for-a-dollar at the "Bargain Basement." Grow an herb garden, or grow some basil and oregano in windowsill pots. It makes for great decor, shaves a nickel or two off the grocery bill, and tastes better fresh anyway!

TAKE A CALCULATOR

Add up the things you toss in your cart. If you see how much you're spending, you won't go over your budget. If you are shopping with a spouse, older kids, or even a roommate, make it a game. Split the list in half and see who can get the best deals, or get everything on their list in the fastest time without going over budget.

EAT LEFTOVERS

Instead of tossing your tuna-noodle casserole down the garbage disposal or leaving it in the fridge to grow a penicillin culture, eat it again for lunch the next day. If it's pizza, eat it for breakfast. The longer you can make your food last, the longer it will be before you have to grocery shop again.

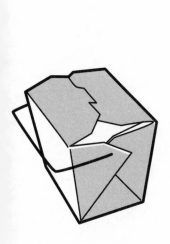

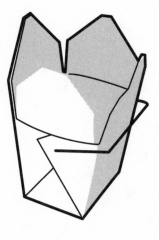

CHEAP WAYS TO INVEST

By Katie Meier

So my sister calls and says, "It's time!" to which I astutely respond, "Um ... time for what?" Apparently she had hoped her seize-the-day excitability would rouse a bit more gusto from her dear-ole sis. After all, she had scrimped and saved and horded and done without, all in anticipation of the day when she was ready to invest. So it came as a surprise when our conversation about investing started with this advice, "Sis, I think you ought'a back your plan on up."

The 2000s brought the world a stumbling U.S. stock market and the revelation that investments can get all "Enron" on us. However, this had little to do with my attitude toward my sister that day. Investing still has fantastic opportunities for those with cash to spend and time to wait. But what investing doesn't have is space for green investors, like my sister, who constantly carry debt. The reasons why are twofold and will serve as our first two ways to invest cheaply.

INVESTING ISN'T LIKE SAVING

Risk takes over when you send dollars to be invested; not everything put in is guaranteed to come back out. When we talk cheap investment ideas, nothing is more cost-free than time, so think, research, and understand that investments are a risk. Calculate whether or not you are poised to take this plunge, both personally and financially. Can you cover the day-to-day without funds that go south for the winter? Do you find yourself in a financial coma after losing nothing more than your spare change in the couch? Do you know "long term" actually means something different in investing than it does in dating? Can you withstand ups and downs, keeping committed to investments over an extended period of time?

INVESTING IS ALL ABOUT RETURNS

If you carry debt, you'll need to make a return on your investment that bests the percentages currently carried on debt to make any money. However, this feat is rarely as easy and breezy as this little sentence sounds. Ten, 15, or even 20 percent interest isn't uncommon for debt loads. Investments that best the double-digit bonanza of interest rates are few and far between. To talk cheap investing, then, is to talk about a return on your money you can count on, and you can find it through debt payoff. Throw the "Naval Gazer's Guide to Investing" out the window and start pouring money into the interest rate drain credit has become on your income. Paying off credit is risk free, and guarantees a return of whatever you put in. For example, paying off $2,500 at 18 percent yields an 18 percent return on that money.

However, not everyone carries debt; not everyone is drained by the debt they do have; not everyone is green to investing. Those who find themselves in these categories can get advice about cheap investing with the following suggestions.

TAKE ADVANTAGE OF TIME

The cheapest investment is one made wisely. Impulse investing or a direction-less approach can be costly in the end. So forget taking stock advice from your uninformed uncle or choosing mutual funds on the advice of those you over-hear on the street. Of course this isn't to say your uncle isn't the most recent incarnation of the work-a-day stock genius, but be smart. Take time on your side and invest after becoming informed about the best choices for your money. Know the difference between a stock and a mutual fund? Know what a market index is, or how an actively managed fund works? Know what kind of profit those who manage your funds make? Know where to find definitions, descriptions, and discussion about investment lingo? The questions could go on and on. Luckily, so does time, making for a tidy equation—and investment—in the end, if you take advantage.

THINK CHEAP, THINK VIRTUAL

Cheap investing can begin without investing at all. From free online programs, to those you can get at your local Comp-u-Store, virtual investing offers a primer in the realities of returns without the risk, or the cost. Here, time spent thinking through the realities of investing can be put to the test. You can feel the heat of the virtual kitchen as you manage make-believe accounts and make decisions about make-believe money. Like those triumphant games of Monopoly where you finally best your arch foe, throwing fake paper money all up in his face, virtual investing offers the same free frills: big money at stake, all of it fake.

B	I	N	G	O
1	24	37	48	61
9	17	42	53	68
6	25	FREE SPACE	69	75
13	25	36	59	74
7	18	31	56	70

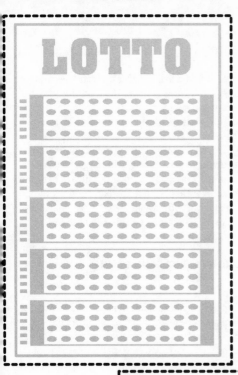

GET IN BEFORE YOU GET PAID

Investing always seems expensive at first when it comes down to the fact that it takes money to make money. Investing isn't about anything but the Benjamins; you've got to give them up to gamble on getting more in return. However, we're an obstinate lot, forever saying we'll save and then returning home with the latest Whip-Bang-Gizmo, only to start in again on our promises come the next pay period. To curb this urge, give in to pretax contributions offered by your employer. Cheap investments are those you can get into little by little. Compensation packages like 401(k) and 403 (b)s take our lil' bits here and there and mash them all together over time. Unlike the Band-Aid we should have just ripped off in one quick motion, with investing it's better (and cheaper) to go bit by bit, allocating where the pieces go over time, rather than plunk a lump-sum down on a potential market loser.

CHEAP IS ACTUALLY A SYNONYM FOR "COMPOUND"

Just as getting in early, and in little bits, can be a cheap way to get big investment returns, waiting for returns to compound is another way to get more for less. Compound returns are highly complex—ready? Your money makes more money over long periods of time. I know, the internal intricacy there was mind-boggling. So perhaps this explains why so many people pay more to invest by perpetually taking out, putting back, taking out, and putting back again the money they've earmarked for investments. Investing cheaply would suggest that we'd like to put the least in and get the most back. But this can't occur if we're ready and willing to pull out our latest profits with every new whim in our lives, because compound returns require, well ... compounding: getting interest, then getting interest on that interest, and interest on the interest on the interest you initially got—get it? Compound returns make investing cheap, but only when you leave the initial amount invested alone.

CHEAP WAYS TO CALL LONG DISTANCE

By Josh Hatcher

Working for a long distance company has taught me oodles about the industry and how it works. When those telemarketers call me and ask me to switch my service, I know what questions to ask about their calling plan to find out if they really plan on saving me money or if they want to rob me blind. The truth is, they are all out to make a buck. If you watch yourself, and listen closely, you can save a ton by not getting caught up into their tricks. You can also avoid using the phone completely. If you want to reach out and touch someone, but don't have money to burn, try these tips.

PLAY THE GAME

The big companies want your business badly, so they offer incentives. They'll send you checks to switch back to their service, or offer you thirty free minutes a month, or lower your rate. If you find two companies that want to fight over you, and keep switching back and forth, you can save a ton. I knew a gal who would switch back and forth from three different carriers every couple of months, and she never paid a cent of long distance, because they would offer her free minutes, or write her a hundred-dollar check.

READ YOUR BILL

Often, we just pay it and don't even look at it, but long distance companies often make mistakes on your bill, or even intentionally add charges to your bill (also called cramming). The FCC regulations are in their favor if you don't respond to any questionable charges within thirty days. Make sure your rates coincide with what they promised you upon sign-up. Find out what taxes and government charges are supposed to be for your state and city, and if they change the name and add their own monthly charges to them. If you notice something fishy and call in to complain about it, and the customer service rep is less than helpful, the key to getting what you want is escalation. Ask for a supervisor. If they cannot help you, ask for a manager. Managers are typically so busy they'll give you anything to get you off the phone, whether they agree with you or not.

KNOW YOUR BILL

There are certain charges that all carriers charge, and most pass it through to their customers. However, many companies make alterations to the charges and lump in enough extra charge to get a kick back. Here are explanations of some of the charges you may see on your long distance bill:

Federal Access Charge (aka: Federal Subscriber Line Charge)

It may be listed as several different names, so watch carefully. Customer Line Charge, Interstate Access Charge, Interstate Single Line Charge, FCC Approved Customer Line Charge, Subscriber Line Charge or SLC are all names that major carriers call this charge. The charge is put out by the local phone company to try to recover some of the cost of installing telephone poles, underground conduit, etc. The FCC does limit the amount that can be charged, and that amount does change every few years. You can find more information at www.fcc.gov. It should only appear on your local phone bill, and if it appears on a long distance bill, you have been crammed.

Monthly Service Fee (aka: Monthly Fee)

Only some carriers charge this fee. It is the one that appears in the fine print underneath the ridiculously low per minute rate. If your long distance rate is four cents per minute, but our monthly fee is five dollars, it may be worth is, if your usage is high enough to recover the monthly fee. But, if you make one call this month, your bill will still contain that monthly fee. If your plan has a monthly fee, it is charged whether you make calls or not.

Monthly Minimum Usage Charge

This charge is structured much like a monthly fee, only conditionally. It is not charged if you meet the minimum requirement for the carrier's calling plan. For example: Your carrier may charge you three dollars for each month that you do not spend a minimum of twenty dollars.

PICC (aka: National Access Fee, Presubscribed Inter-exchange Carrier Charge, Presubscribed Line Charge, Regulatory Related Charge, or Carrier Line Charge)

This is a charge that is very similar to the Federal Access Charge, in that it is an FCC approved charge to reover the costs for local loops. However, as of July 2000, the FCC determined that Single line business and residential lines should not be charged. This fee should only be assessed on business lines, where there is more than one phone line. However, some carriers still charge this to their residential customers, and the money goes directly to their pockets.

USF (aka: Universal Service Fund Charge or Universal Service Charge)

This charge is a percentage of your interstate and international usage. The Government taxes the carrier for such a charge, and then the carrier splits it up amongst their customers. The money from this goes to recover the cost of providing telephone service to libraries, rural health care providers, and educational facilities. Carriers can set their own amount to charge their customers. One carrier may charge more than another. Although the percentage is an extremely low amount, it might be good to keep an eye on the charge to make sure it stays in control.

PEAK HOURS

Some plans have peak hours where the rates are the lowest, like free nights and weekends or five-cent Sundays. Just make your long distance calls on those days. Only call during non-peak hours when absolutely necessary. If you let your boyfriend in Wisconsin know that you are only going to call him on Sundays, or after 7 P.M., I'm sure he'll be there waiting for your call. The same is true with family and friends. Make an appointment to call them when your rates are cheaper.

THE INTERNET

Don't call when you can e-mail or use an instant messenger. Some instant messengers (like MSN) actually allow you to talk using your computer's microphone and speakers, just like a speakerphone. With all this groundbreaking technology right on our desktops, we could cut our long distance bills down to a few dollars each month.

CELL PHONES

I have a friend who only calls me from his car. He has to have a cell phone for work, and he chose free long distance as one of his options. The only time he ever calls long distance is while he's driving down the road with his cell phone (which is illegal in New York state). If you don't need a cell phone, it wouldn't be worth the extra money each month for a cellular bill. But if you have to have one anyway, get a plan with free options.

LOOK IT UP

Directory Assistance is making billions on laziness. Dig out your phone book; leave it by the phone. Use the Internet to look up out of town numbers. Two great sites for directory assistance are *www.switchboard.com* and *www.any-who.com*. If you have to use directory assistance, be sure to have a pen and paper with you before you call. When they offer to dial the number automatically, they are charging people a chunk and a half.

PHONE HOME

When you're at a pay phone and you need to get in touch with someone, it helps if you memorize your calling card number. It may be more expensive than the pay phone service, but it is definitely cheaper than calling collect. Calling collect can rack up the charges faster than anything. If you don't have fifty cents in your pocket, it's not worth it to add five dollars to your phone bill next month by calling collect. Any collect calls that you make have minimum usage charges, and they can get extremely pricey.

CHEAP WAYS TO BE IN DEBT
By Katie Meier

If you're already in debt, it's likely that you could do without another lecture about the woes of credit. So instead, we'll get straight to the show. Below you'll find ways you can be in debt for now, for cheap, and find a bit of inspiration for hanging in there and taking your balance down to zero.

IT TAKES A STRETCH TO PAY DEBT DOWN

Though it will surely come sooner than the next time the planets align or the next Macarena phenomenon, the magical moment when you reach a zero dollar balance could be some time off. In the meantime, work on getting interest rates down as low as possible, a task that doesn't take a genius—or a magician—to pull off. If you want a lower rate, just ask. Of course, success isn't guaranteed. Rates aren't likely to budge if you're already sporting single-digit interest numbers. And for those who are perpetually late on payments or a sorry credit risk to begin with, don't get your hopes up. Creditors cut slack for customers they want to keep, not for those with whom they have to hassle just to rein in a payment. So consider whether you're worthy, but keep two mottos in mind: "It can't hurt to ask" and "'no' really means call back and talk to a different customer rep on a different day."

DEBT LIKES TO SEE NEW PLACES, DO NEW THINGS

Don't settle for letting debt stay in one place its whole life. After all, debt wants to see the world too, and you'll benefit by being an indulgent parent and moving debt around. Balance transfer programs can keep debt cheap as they offer months of low-to-no interest on money moved over from some other part of town. But creditors don't ask you to play on their block for long; you can usually move your money when low interest rates are at the cusp of being raised. Read the fine print to be sure, but playing the game of "who's-my-best-credit-friend?" can make debt fairly cheap. Just be sure to pay on time, and to pay more than the minimum. That way, the money you're sending won't be tainted with penalties and will go straight to the balances you're trying to pay down rather than walk off to the land of interest.

LOW INTEREST LOANS

From school loans you can get to ensure that course fees don't end up on the credit card, to personal loans you can get across the street at Bank of Any-Town, USA, be sure to use low interest loans to keep expenses cheap. Though one should question the practices of those who perpetually live life in the red, debt is often the result of a life spent in the pursuit of the practically normal these days, like a car or a college degree. To get these debts down to their cheapest levels, sick a low interest loan on 'em. For example, a credit union connected to your work might offer a loan rate well below the one you were offered two years ago, when the blazing—and perhaps hypnotic?!—summer heat radiated so hot off the pavement it caused you to blurt out, "Whatever financing sounds fine—just wrap the car up!" Fix such blunders in good judgment, and get your debt down cheap by paying a loan with a loan.

STAY AWAY FROM "GRADUATED" SCHEDULES

Debt isn't cheap when it goes on and on. Because lenders have made some debt—like school loans—eligible for ever longer terms of repayment, the number of times people will pay on this debt now rivals only the number of times certain stars will go under the knife. If you think Jacko and his fellow surgery-prone friends get scarier with each new adjustment, just imagine what your debt must look like under the same conditions. Graduated repayment schedules subject our debt to a type of surgery by continually remaking its face. Because payments start small and get bigger over time, the face of our debt—and interest—is ever changing, with the bulk of the payoff lasting for the long term. For example, a debt of $15,000 at 8.25 percent will first cost about $100 a month, and gradually rise to a cost of a bit more than $200. The result of all this adjusting over time is interest ... nearly $14,000 worth, not a nit-picky-nothing little amount. Paying straight on the debt would have cost about $180 per month, but saves somewhere in the ballpark of $7,000 in interest over time. So make haste to get away from graduated payments if you're looking to get debt cheap.

CONDITIONAL CONSOLIDATION

There are two types of consolidation we're talking about here: credit counseling/debt consolidation and loan consolidation. In the former debt scenario, we'll likely find that consolidation companies can be awfully kind when we're debtors who've gone so far in the hole that all we're looking for is a way to get along in the world for cheap, because our only other option seems to be default or bankruptcy. Consolidation companies cover us by getting bills—like credit, medical, school, or taxes—under control by restructuring our debt. In effect, debt consolidation programs serve as middlemen who contact and negotiate with our creditors to reorganize our outstanding debts, lower interest rates, and centralize payments. This allows our credit problems to move more quickly toward being paid away, thereby offering us a lower cost of being in debt over time. Between consolidation and bankruptcy, though both can blight your credit, consolidation should reign king as you don't default and get your debt paid off with an eye toward the cheap.

In the latter debt scenario, loan consolidation, one word will suffice: math. Being in debt for school, for example, only comes cheap if the lower monthly payment you'll get through consolidation doesn't extend the life of the loan out too far. Lower interest rates and/or monthly payments that turn a seven-year payback plan into a thirty-year one, for example, aren't actually cheaper if a higher rate/higher payment plan would extinguish the debt sooner (perpetual payments on even low interest debt add up if you continue to pay them for enough time). Debt always costs more than payoff, so figure the cost of the loan with high and low interest payment scenarios to see which is actually cheaper in the long run.

CHEAP WAYS TO START SAVING

By Katie Meier

The act of saving money is nearly an antiquity in the modern world. And because I've found my banter about this subject is nearly as popular as munching on Spam is on people's top 15,000 list of favorite pastimes, suggestions for saving are often hard to recommend. So I'll leave the bar charts that track personal saving habits since the time of Saturday Night Fever-style disco to say it all: while all manner of terrible trends were increasing—from tight-fitting pants for men to sparkly headbands—the trend toward personal saving was decidedly on the decline.

Not surprisingly, this decline mirrored the rise of MasterCard and others who formed international banking affiliations to offer the keys of credit to consumers far and wide. Cheap ways to start saving begins with a reverse of this history, by leaving credit debt, low collective savings rates, and those tight-fitting trousers behind.

MAKE YOUR BALANCE DISAPPEAR

The cheapest savings plan is one that you'll never see. The fortunes generated by creditors are made by charging interest, an "invisible" fee for using their services. Though you never see the money you're losing, don't doubt this money goes away. With every check you send to cover the balances that remain, a portion of the money goes to cover interest, and thus is lost from both your actual payment and your pocketbook. To get savings on the cheap, then, take this money back. Without a balance, you can't lose money to interest, so pay off what you owe to save yourself the "invisible" fees.

FOLLOW THE MASTERCARD MODEL

Creditors aren't all bad; after all, they exhibit the best in traits toward saving money cheaply: they collect over time, they never give up, and they never go away. If you're all too familiar with the truth of this statement, get to reenacting it in your daily life; finding cheap ways to save starts by becoming a copycat. The cheapest savings plan begins with the tenacity to contribute tiny amounts over time. Think two dollars, ten dollars, twenty dollars or even loose coins at the end of the day don't add up over time? If you're still in disbelief, check the mail and look at that minimum payment again. It's all about collecting little bits over a long, long time.

FOLLOW THE CORPORATE MODEL

Employers aren't lying when they push the 401(k) packet forward and say, "This is the best deal you're ever gonna get!" Most employers offer a match (free money for every dollar you put in) making deferred retirement plans a sure bet when it comes to saving money. However, when it comes to saving cheap, the plan also helps us out as it gives us the right to decide just how much of our paycheck we'd like to put aside. Want to start saving on the cheap? Get crackin' with a 1 percent deduction, as even pennies put aside will be money well spent.

STOP SPENDING ON STUPID STUFF

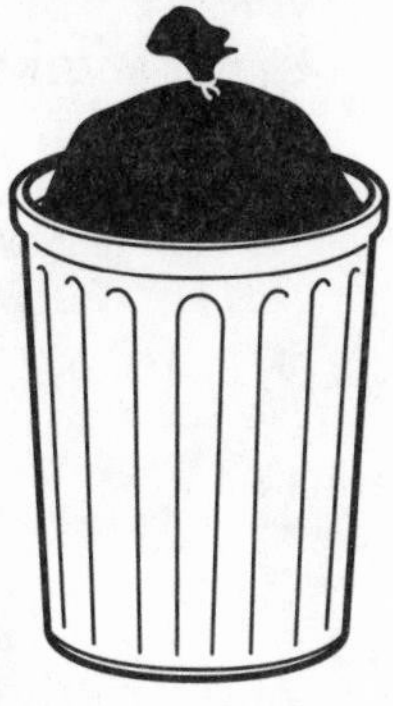

STOP SPENDING ON STUPID STUFF

Not that you don't actually read *Extreme Fisherman*, but the cost of the magazine itself could compound over time to be worth more than the fishing boats pictured within. "Stupid stuff" is a space in the budget from which funds seem to never return, a black hole of sorts that eats money available for saving at the same rate as broken-down spacecrafts and other extraterrestrial trash.

Stupid stuff comes in two categories: stuff we buy, and stuff we subscribe to or pay for throughout the year. For example, the infomercial-advertised Ab-Flex or your daily Starbucks might fall under the former, while a homeowners warranty might fall under the latter; after all, if you're paying $500 a year to cover the cost of repairing appliances, you'll need to replace about an appliance a year to make up for the premium you're paying.

START SAVING THE SMALL STUFF

Everyone receives a boon to his or her income from time to time. You may not think the ten-dollar rebate for that seventy-pack of toilet paper counts, but you should. Saving the little stuff over a long period of time can really add up, and it's a cheap way to get started, as the least expensive way to get anything in life is to use other people's money. So whether it's a refund from a product at your local Jumbo-Mart or a birthday gift from Aunt Minnie, take a portion for yourself to spend, but look to saving the bulk of these little income bonuses received over time.

GET CREATIVE WITH YOUR INCOME TAXES

To brag about the amount we get in return each year has become tantamount to bragging about the Porsche, mansion, or bling-bling we've bought to show our savvy to the world. Unfortunately, as those who drive beaten-down Volvos know from actually attending econ class, the money that's returned is simply our own. We're not making any money off the government when we sport a fat return check. In fact, getting money back is a sign that we've overpaid our share of tax, effectively giving the government a one-year loan, interest free.

This situation can be interpreted in two ways: (1) The government has been good, nice enough to store my money all neat and safe for me; (2) The government has been bad, taken my money, and collected for itself interest I could have been making myself. Looking through each lens, here is what the situation can mean in terms of getting savings cheap:

(1) If the government saves the money, any interest to be made is lost but the money is babysat, and thus safe from those with spendthrift ways. To "ask" the government to save even more for you, adjust the specifics of your W4 in either the Personal Allowances or Deductions and Adjustments sections. Then take the aforementioned advice and bank the money that comes your way after you file each April; if you haven't needed the cash all year, surely it's safe enough to put it away to save. (2) If the government is making interest on the money, I could be doing the same, provided I can keep the most money possible for myself each year. Here we go back to the W4 as you'll need to adjust your withholding accordingly, to come as close as you can to getting zero dollars back after April in order to keep cash—and interest—to yourself.

CHEAP WAYS TO GET HEALTH INSURANCE By Katie Meier

If you have only a faint memory of your last visit to the doctor and are fairly sure the event ended with a sparkly sticker and a sucker, it's likely you've been divorced from decent insurance for some time and are looking to stay away from medical care unless you notice one day that you've lost a limb or two. Don't despair if this predicament describes you to a tee. Here are some suggestions for getting care without a ton of cost—and for getting care that's worth what you'll pay.

A PENNY FOR YOUR THOUGHTS

Thoughts are only good as an exchange on cash when we put our brainpower to work in real life. Each thought toward considering the type, frequency, location, or style of healthcare you want can be worth a fortune over time; such thinking allows you to specify exactly which services are necessary and which can fall by the wayside, leaving your wallet a bit fatter with cash. Without a concise compilation of healthcare needs, plans are picked willy-nilly, a situation that can have you paying for services you'll never use. Pay attention to policy coverage, as you may be covered for more than you need. Likewise, attention to exclusion clauses can save cash if you catch them before you're forced to pay out-of-pocket.

READ THE INGREDIENTS

Employers often cover the total cost of healthcare for employees. That is employees who pick the cheapest package, who don't have children, who don't have a spouse, who don't do this or that or do two-dozen of the other. To make employer-allocated funds go further, read about and compare all choices, charting them over one year.

For example, Plan Seems-Like-You-Don't-Pay features a zero dollar deductible for all in-patient services. This plan costs an additional forty dollars per month, and is offered side-by-side with Plan Pay-A-Lump-Sum, a package that has no additional monthly fee but features a one-time deductible of $350 for all in-patient services. A quick consideration of the two plans over the course of a year tells the tale: Plan Pay-A-Lump-Sum costs $350 to use, while Plan Seems-Like-You-Don't-Pay actually costs $130 more, as the extra forty dollars per month in premiums comes to a yearly cost of $480. Same service, very different cost.

You can also save on care by reading up on employer-sponsored "flex spending" accounts that allow you to put pre-tax money aside for medical coverage. Rather than lose portions of your paycheck to Uncle Sam because the money put out for coverage comes after tax, look into flex accounts to keep this money for yourself.

DON'T DOUBLE UP

Though more is usually perceived as better, here more is just more; an extra helping of the same means double fees for the same coverage options. To be sure how much insurance or coverage you need, check out how much you might already have in other places. For example, worker's compensation, or state regulated aid, covers medical expenses due to disability or death sustained while in the performance of an employee's duties. Provided the injury is an accident and not due to intoxication, employers provide some medical coverage for disability or death. Thus, a personal healthcare plan that charges to provide the same kind of injury accident coverage might be money spent twice.

PLAN FOR THE CYCLES OF YOUR LIFE

While emergencies are unexpected, other needs occur regularly. From birth control to gynecological exams to physicals or prescription drugs, regular services should be considered a vital part of a healthcare plan. Without coverage for what occurs on a regular basis, we ask to pay the highest price for our care, as out-of-pocket expenses can eat away at even the biggest budgets. In addition, be realistic about the potentials in your life and plan for them as well. For example, a woman on birth control has some likelihood of conceiving a child. A plan to have protected sex should make room for the potential of pregnancy, as adding or adjusting healthcare options can be costly after the fact.

SHOP AROUND

When you've decided what needs you'd like to spend your funds providing, be sure to shop those needs around, if you can. Just like your local Quick-N-Shop keeps prices high on items unless you fill out the form and chain yourself to one of their plastic bar code coupon cards, healthcare companies have been known to do the same. Various companies have various levels of commitment, styles of coverage, services, or prescription plans, each tailored to a different consumer. Just like the Quick-N-Shop then, find the store (company) that suits your tastes best, as each company caters to a slightly different crowd (students, retirees, elderly, etc.) and provides better plastic-coupon style deals for different types of service (personal doctors vs. covered groups of physicians).

CHECK THE MAPS; KNOW THE ROUTES

Healthcare offers provision for injury, illness, and all manner of other bodily harm provided you seek treatment "in network." To get the cheapest care, you'll have to stay inside these boundaries or ask permission, real nice-like, to wander a bit astray. Doctors, hospitals, and urgent care facilities are all designated by the insurance plan you choose, and while you may have a wealth of options in each of these areas, costs skyrocket when you order off the menu, so to speak. So know your network well and keep inside its bounds.

"HEALTHY" IS A SYNONYM FOR CHEAP

While this last recommendation has little to do with the actual cost of a health-care plan, the cheapest healthcare is healthcare you don't need. A healthy lifestyle can keep costs down as the likelihood that you'll develop expensive health conditions—from diabetes to lung cancer to liver problems—over the course of your lifetime is dramatically reduced. Also reduced is the tendency to fall prey to genetic diseases made apparent (or worse) through poor health or excess weight. Keep the machine that is your body in good condition if you expect to keep it free from costly repairs.

CHEAP WAYS TO GET LEGAL HELP
By Katie Meier

There's nothing more common than a snotty comeback or slight after publicly admitting any affiliation with law or the lawyers who practice it. From the paralegal who's sent flowers on Secretary's Day, to the unwillingness of anyone to listen to science (or reason) and actually classify those who practice law as a mammal rather than one of those Great White fish, those in the legal field often receive less-than-stellar treatment despite the fact that their services remain in high demand.

However, personally significant situations can arise, situations so sticky—or sensitive—that we're forced to ask for help and seek legal aid. As we set out to chart this territory, the first order of business for keeping this task cheap is to understand just whom we're seeing and how much these people cost.

LAWYER VS. PARALEGAL

"Lawyer" is often a generalized term for those who hold a degree, are specialists in law, and are licensed to perform various legal functions on our behalf. Though we're technically speaking of an attorney, in either case we understand the individual to be qualified and licensed. In pursuit of legal aid, then, consider what you seek when you ask for a lawyer—a trained professional who has earned both a law degree and a valid license to practice. Such a history proba-bly won't come cheap.

On the other hand, a "paralegal" is someone with specialized training in law, who assists an attorney, understands the legal process, and is legally able to offer services such as "document preparation" in many states but has neither a specialized degree in law nor a license to practice in the field. Thus, if your legal needs fall within the bounds of a paralegal's capacity, you'll likely pay less than you would if a lawyer handled the same situation. But keep in mind the cheapest legal help is good help that makes the problem go away in a succinct fashion. Without a reputable and competent paralegal, seemingly small problems can explode, get messy, and require the clean-up work of a lawyer after the fact. If this occurs, the mess of it all can cost much more than you would have shelled out initially for a lawyer to take it from the top.

USE FREE TIME TO MAKE TIME FREE

After understanding the connection between whom we seek and the expense of that individual, the next way to curb legal costs is to spend our free time finding ways to become educated. Because time is money in the world of law, and all of the money spent will be yours since you'll foot the final bill, cut down on the chit-chat each time you go through the in-office meet and greet. The world of online information can make this education a reality; websites like *www.FindLaw.com*, or *www.(My State's Initials)Bar.org* can lead you through the pertinents of your situation, case, or legal concern, cutting significant sums off the final bill by shortening expensive Q&A conversations for which you'll be billed.

And for those who want to carry some of this education further, try lessening legal costs by filling out the flurry of legal forms yourself. If you live in a state supporting self-help or do-it-yourself centers for legal matters, the combination of these service centers with laws like "no fault" divorce makes matters of legality only about 326 questions, four pages, and two signatures away. More work for you, but would it be a real encounter with cheap service any other way? A quick call to your local court can tell you where (or whether) these services exist around you.

COMMUNITY MEANS CHEAP

Another route to reduced legal aid is the non-profit in your local community. Though these organizations are generally for the indigent or those in circumstances of catastrophe such as fire, murder, or other weighty situations of life, volunteer legal aid is something to inspect. Many community legal aid centers/non-profits specialize in work for the average John and Jane, provided he or she has particular legal problems. From spousal abuse concerns to renter's rights to coverage for the aging and the elderly, particular populations and problems will qualify for various levels of cheap (or free) legal aid.

In addition, be sure to ask community and non-profit legal centers for any references they have for lawyers who do pro bono work, either through the center or on their own as a service to the community. For those unfamiliar with the term, "pro bono" basically translates into the provision of legal services for those who cannot otherwise afford to hire an attorney. Pro bono work, if you can get it, is a great way to go if a qualified candidate comes calling to serve on your behalf, as fees are often slashed to zero or considerably reduced in order to offer equal justice to those without fat funds.

GO BACK TO COLLEGE

Any accredited school featuring a law program is bound to have among its members staff or faculty who are still practicing attorneys. From the institutes these individuals run in order to reach out to others through cheap legal advice, to the fingers-crossed chance that your situation might rustle the heartstrings of a professor on sabbatical or other break from teaching, perusing local universities and colleges may turn up some good leads toward getting legal aid on the cheap.

CHEAP BUT CONDITIONAL

If you're flat-out broke, laid up because of that nasty little injury accident, and on the couch watching Jerry Springer, it's likely you know where this last suggestion is going. From the side of that downtown bus to you, let me introduce J.J. Sullivan and Sons ... Attorneys Who Will Fight For You! Here legal aid can be had through a "contingency fee," the practice of giving up nothing but a big, healthy cut of the final outcome of your lawsuit. This arrangement is helpful for those who are flat broke, but should be considered "cheap" only on this condition. In the end, the sum you'll pay for contingency is high: 25 to 40 percent. So, contingency is a way to go depending on your predicament and on your perception of the word "cheap."

CHEAP WAYS TO MAKE EXTRA MONEY

By Katie Meier

If you're one to consider the couch a main artery in the heart of your yearly income, then the fabric burns on your face will tell the sorry tale of hard won quarters and dimes, almost too deep to reach. Fear not, however, if you've searched endlessly for other options, as the suggestions below might be an addition boon to your income.

TAKE A KITCHEN ON THE ROAD

For the minimal cost of time, labor, and ingredients, you can whip up a batch of Great Aunt Mildred's Colossal Cookies and get something in return. Set up shop near a local swap or flea market, or sell foodstuff on the local garage sale circuit. If you're not the type to hail from a culinary-inclined family, you can take the "Little League" route and stock up on standard Saturday-type items from your local Super-Mart, and then simply mark up on each. Cold cans of pop and the promise of pre-packaged sweets has had the suburban set for years, as moms, dads, daughters, and the occasional passersby fill park after park each weekend to follow the sporting achievements of their family and friends. Because these sporting adventures often star athletes as young as four, the sports are turned into slow-paced spin-offs of the originals, leaving families everywhere stuck to the sidelines for what can seem like days. Be advised, dire thirst and hunger can follow such events; just set yourself up in a space that takes advantage.

GROSS BUT GOOD FOR SOMETHING

Though the sight of blood, or any other bodily fluid, is enough to send the squeamish running from the room, those who can stand the heat can get out of the kitchen with some cash. By donating to those in need, through agencies like the Red Cross and others, you can get paid and someone else can get, well, lots of things. From blood to semen to plasma and beyond, someone needs the extra fluid you can spare. To donate is to allow others to conceive, heal, and be made well in surgery or other situations. So while others say, "Gross!" say instead, "Sign me up for some extra cash and perhaps some O.J. and cookies on the house."

TRIED, TRUE, AND WORTH SOMETHING TO SOMEONE : JUNK

It's been said before, and we'll say it again: One person's junk is another person's treasure. Of course we've all seen the suits, books, blenders, and old baby toys for sale each weekend at neighborhood garage sales. But some of this junk can go farther in cyber space, reaching out to those who simply can't live without—and will pay a bundle for—the plastic Pillsbury Dough Boy you sent away for so long ago after seeing the ad on the side of that Poppin' Crescents container sitting in the fridge. Internet auction sites such as eBay make this process easy, as they allow you to photograph your junk and post it online for public consumption. The highest bidder wins, paying you a tidy little sum, and then you send him or her the Pillsbury Dough Boy figurine of his or her dreams.

SIT THROUGH A BUNCH OF BULL

You'll find yourself saying, "No thanks," all day long, but you'll come out ahead if you can just hold out long enough to collect on your investment. From time-share plans to all-inclusive vacation packages, people long to pay for a willing audience to hawk their products. One-day and weekend sales seminars can bring profit to those who attend for nothing more than an investment of time and patience. Though the profit you'll likely make will be paid in trade or comps at local businesses and restaurants, an outing to a sales pitch featuring freebies can be an interesting change from starting with lots and ending with none as you spend a day or night on the town.

SELL YOUR NOTES

Have organizational skills at hand? You may be able to make some money by doing something you already do—take notes. Collegiate disability resource centers often help students in need by featuring a note-taking service that allows students more time to concentrate on the lecture because someone else took all the notes. Be this person and you can turn time you have to spend in class anyway into a profit-making venture. Check the center on your campus for specifics, but nearly all centers require this type of service and are willing to send money your way if you'll volunteer to simply do what you already do, plus a bit of Xeroxing.

GET ALL MEDIEVAL ON 'EM

Just because it isn't the year of our Lord 1153 and you don't know anyone named Geoffrey of Clairvaux doesn't mean the barter system is dead. Cheap income can come in trade, from CDs to clothes to books to old band equipment. Take the items you'll never use again and swap them out at various stores for a new round of delights. Also, consider trading services. Look decidedly modern by getting truly old school about it, and trade your skill set for another for which you'd have to pay. Fix someone's piano in return for two week's worth of fresh baked bread, or offer computer consulting for a swap on that clunkity-clunk noise your car keeps making. And, keep in mind the trade-for-play idea if you're into sports or other adventure outlets. Mind a bike shop for free, get a spot on their cross-country trek of canyons in America, or get yourself on the green of your dreams by offering to caddy for free a few days a week on that course.

GRAB BAG

Get your car to work for you by charging for carpool service. Play the old recycle game—get cash on your empties. Work overtime, after all you're already there. Play all the games you can. Clip and (try to) win on every wrapper, box, bag, and container you come across. Go out and ask. Imagine if everyone you know would just play along and give you one dollar.

CHEAP WAYS TO LIVE BELOW YOUR MEANS By Katie Meier

If you're like me, you don't consider yourself a consumer glutton. You don't own the road with your pimped-out Excursion. You don't own the neighborhood with your seven-bedroom mansion. Nope, you're just a little piece of the American pie. You take in a few dinners and movies with your friends, you drive whatever you can afford—and will get you there—and when you splurge it's rarely on a private jet or a gold-plated hot tub.

But whether we buy the bling-bling or the boring, we need to recognize that we all have the potential to become consumer gluttons. To live a life below our means is less about the amount we consume than knowing what our limits of consumption are, or what they should be. Best the prototypical picture of a life lived in debt and beyond your budget by checking out the advice below.

KEEP RECEIPTS

Consider keeping receipts cheap therapy, as it works in two annoyingly effective ways: (1) It's a big-ole pain. The more we're forced to endure the asking, collecting, and saving that go with stashing receipts, the more aware we're forced to become aware about our spending. (2) It's a running tally right in front of our face. It will only take a few receipts to tell how closely related we're becoming to Sir Elton (Did I mention his bankruptcy problems?).

CULTIVATE CONCIOUSNESS

To become conscious spenders, here's what we need to do: take the aforementioned advice about receipts, and get realistic about earning versus spending. First, take one week and actually keep receipts from all the stuff you buy and all the bills you pay. Second, get out the calculator, sit down with a cold beverage (you kept the receipt for that beverage, right?), relax, and add up the damage. Next, find your last paycheck and divide this amount (by two or four) to understand exactly how much you make each week of your life. Last, and most magical of all, compare the total you spend with the total you pull in.

Doing this over the course of one month will likely walk you straight into the honest fact that you're overspent and using credit to cover you. A change in lifestyle costs nothing and can have you living within your means in no time.

FORGET LUMP-SUM LIVING

Do envelopes, do a money program, do whatever, just abandon a life lived by the lump-sum balance in your bankbook. Lump-sum living is too tempting and too vague, a sure sign of something that might lead us away from a life lived under our means. Instead, introduce (dut da da da!) "Spending Sectors" into your life. From CDs to collectables, from groceries to Grande Mochaccinos, spending sectors make you a diva of divvying funds, and at the same time set limits on spending. Set sector limits by allocating funds to each. Spending is fine, but sectors clear up the picture and keep you from capitalizing on the longings only lump-sum living can provide.

CHEAP OUT ON THE EVERYDAY

Though we use some services over and over everyday, we rarely check back over time to insure that we're still getting a good deal. If you still think a free toaster is what banking is all about, it's time to get with the times, pop. Check your bank, phone, insurance, cable, cell, and other service providers to be sure you're getting the cheapest rates, rather than paying inflated fees for old school options, services, or allocations of coverage. In addition, get your head out of the clouds with regard to your real life; though the 1977 Nissan might be a superstar in your eyes, premium gas and that weekly wash and wax can bend a budget to the max over the course of time. Let items absorb costs appropriate to their stature and with regard to the reality of your means.

DON'T KEEP UP WITH THE JONESES

They might have the tight ride and the sweet crib, but they're likely in debt and living well beyond their means. End the rivalry of ridiculous stuff by providing for yourself what you can afford and no more. Learn from the wisdom of pop music here and realize, "It's not having what you want, it's wanting what you've got."

LEARN ABOUT DEBT RATIOS

Living below our means might seem to have everything to do with saving, but it's actually about learning how to spend with some precision; after all, from college degrees to cul-de-sac homes, there will always be a few things nearly everyone will have to go into debt in order to provide. Thus, living below our means when carrying debt has to do with understanding how much debt we can take on—too much debt and our budget will bend so far out of whack we'll think we're a bunch of old ladies trying to do the electric slide.

Figure your "debt ratio" to see if your budget is becoming "loaned out," so to speak, by having taken on too many creditors. Because a debt ratio is just your total monthly debt payments divided by your monthly income, it's easy to figure. Anything more than 40 percent is a sign you're likely in too deep to maintain a life below your means and could be headed for a serious financial fiasco soon.

SUGGESTIONS WILLY-NILLY

Make a wish list of items and ask for them as gifts to cut costs. Pay for things that are planned or necessary expenses only by making emergencies, extras, and seasonal splurges a part of your regular budget, not an afterthought you afford through credit. Impose a waiting period on all major purchases rather than falling prey to impulse buying, and save for the item bit-by-bit while you wait. Don't buy on credit; if you do, write a check for the cost and deduct it from your account that same day to be certain you don't let interest get the better of you when you can't pay the balance at the end of the month.

ABOUT THE AUTHORS

Jason Boyett is a writer, musician, and occasional artist whose work has appeared in a variety of print and online publications. He is creative director for a marketing, design, and communications company in Amarillo, Texas.

Margaret Feinberg is a writer based in Steamboat Springs, Colorado. She is author of *God Whispers: Learning to Hear His Voice* and a contributing writer to both *Enjoying God: Embracing Intimacy with the Heavenly Father* and I AM RELEVANT. When she is not writing, she can be found enjoying the Colorado outdoors hiking, skiing, and snowshoeing.

Josh Hatcher is the father of three small children, and the husband of a hardworking stay-at-home mom in rural Pennsylvania. He is a freelance writer, graphic designer, musician, and youth leader.

Katie Meier has published two books, a bevy of articles, and her artwork has most recently appeared on the cover of *Panic: Origins, Insight, and Treatment*, by Brooke Warner. Katie lives in the southwest with her husband where she is currently completing a graduate degree in religion.